BEHIND *the* SCENES

The Way *of the* Master

THE AWARD-WINNING TELEVISION SERIES
with KIRK CAMERON & RAY COMFORT

genesis
PUBLISHING GROUP

Presented to:

....

By:

....

Behind the Scenes: "The Way of the Master"

Genesis Publishing Group
2002 Skyline Place
Bartlesville, OK 74006
www.genesis-group.net

Photography by Carol J. Scott, CJ Studio, Covina, CA (www.cj-studio.com)

Edited by Lynn Copeland

Cover, page design, and production by Genesis Group

Photographs on page 97 of the Cerritos Library © Marcus Tate (mtspace@sisna.com). Used by permission

Printed in the United States of America

ISBN 0-9749300-2-4

*For more information about "The Way of the Master"
or other resources by Kirk Cameron and Ray Comfort, contact:*

The Way of the Master
P.O. Box 1172
Bellflower, CA 90706
www.wayofthemaster.com
877-496-8688

Preface

FOR MANY YEARS I prayed that one day God would trust me to preach at large crusades. This was because I noticed that some mass crusades had great untapped evangelistic potential. Let's say that two hundred churches combined to host a crusade. Of the 100,000 people there on the opening night, more than likely 80 to 90 percent would be professing Christians. Statistics reveal that most of these people (as many as 98 percent) don't share their faith, so it made sense to me that, as an evangelist, I should be "equipping the saints for the work of ministry" (Ephesians 4:11,12). With God's help, my vision was to challenge those who professed to love God about their lack of evangelistic concern, and then teach them how to share their faith. D. L. Moody said, "I would rather set a thousand to work, than do the work of a thousand." Billy Graham stated, "Mass crusades, to which I have devoted my life, will not do the job. But one to one will." Then I would preach the gospel to the unsaved at the crusade.

It seems that God heard my heart's prayer. In October 2001, when Kirk Cameron listened to my teaching called "Hell's Best Kept Secret" and contacted our ministry, I had no idea what would unfold.

In January 2003, after Kirk shared the teaching on a major Christian television network, our website received over a million hits in one day! The network's ratings went through the roof, so they asked him to regularly host their program. Kirk instead suggested that we produce a program teaching Christians how to share their faith, and that they air it. They loved the idea, and "The Way of the Master" television show was born.

The weekly program reaches far more than a mere

100,000 people in a stadium. It has begun to air on multiple networks, in over 70 countries, and is viewed by millions.

I am amazed at how everything came together to make this a reality. For instance, I liked our director/producer Duane Barnhart from the moment I met him in the late 1990s. He was the director of a film crew who had flown from Florida to California to do a number of shoots for a television program. One of those programs was "Hell's Best Kept Secret."

After filming, we remained friends and stayed in contact, and I eventually asked him to come to work for our ministry. He told me later that that had been his heart's desire since we met.

Then there was Ron Meade, our editor/cameraman. He showed up at our ministry to buy some books just as an eighteen-wheeler backed into our parking lot. As we began to unload boxes, Ron enthusiastically joined in and worked like a horse. His diligent work ethic so impressed me, I asked him to join the ministry.

Stuart and Carol Scott (sound/still photography) showed up every Friday night for over a year as I preached open-air in Santa Monica. Over time I got to know them, and grew to love them.

Anna ("Banana") Jackson lived in Ohio and did voluntary work on our website. When Kirk and I spoke in her area, she handed me her résumé, saying she believed she was going to work for the ministry. I didn't even open it, as

I didn't think we had a need. But she proved to be such a talented webmaster, we decided to employ her full-time here in California.

A few weeks before Anna and her husband, Dale, left Ohio, he slipped on some ice and seriously hurt his back. I knew that he was involved in some sort of design work at his job, but I didn't know that he was a graphic artist. When he moved to California, the only way he could stay with his employer was to drive trucks for them. I empathized with him because of his injured back, and decided that he could also work for the ministry. I put him in Anna's office. I had no idea that he was such a brilliant graphic artist and that he had the talent he has to create movie graphics.

Neither did I know that Scotty was a sound expert, or that Carol had studied professional photography, or that Ron worked for Hollywood's prestigious film company, Dreamworks.

So when I look on our talented team, I can see God's hand in bringing them together. Add the celebrity and talents of Kirk Cameron, and you have "The Way of the Master."

Each photo in this book brings back very fond memories (and many laughs). I hope that they will also bring you pleasure and that the articles and insights encourage you in your endeavors to reach out more effectively to this dying world.

Until the nets are full,

We give ourselves to prayer. We preach a gospel that saves to the uttermost, and we witness to its power. We do not argue about worldliness; we witness. We do not discuss philosophy; we preach the gospel. We do not speculate about the destiny of sinners; we pluck them as brands from the burning. We ask no man's patronage. We beg no man's money. We fear no man's frown. Let no man join us who is afraid, and we want none but those who are saved, sanctified, and aflame.

—Samuel Chadwick

Episodes

VIEWER'S QUESTION

"Since the show is filmed in so many varied and interesting locations, indoors and out, how do you decide where to go each week?"

We originally had our graphic artist design a beautiful indoor set, but our producer, Duane Barnhart, suggested it would be unique to have a different location for each episode. We all loved the idea, and it has helped to make the show fresh and appealing.

We are always on the lookout for unusual locations. For example, let's say we decided to film in a lighthouse, because we heard a true story of a lighthouse keeper who gave fuel to passing ships that ran out of fuel. When a storm came, he ran out of fuel himself, because he had given it away. His light therefore went out, a ship ran aground, and people tragically drowned. His own kindnesses caused him to be unfaithful to his primary task. How that sums up the Church—doing good works, while failing to warn the lost of the rocks of eternal judgment. So we would then search for an appropriate lighthouse and begin the process of gaining permission, acquiring the necessary filming permits, and handling travel logistics.

One big problem with a location that is hundreds of miles away is that someone who understands the ins and outs of filming has to go there to scout out filming angles, etc. It is very unwise to set up a shoot without scouting it beforehand. For instance, we were planning to film "The Satanic

Influence" program in a cave just north of Los Angeles. The day before the shoot, authorities found a crack in the cave and deemed it unsafe. Someone suggested another location, but when we scouted it out on the day of the shoot, the ground was found to be too steeply sloped to set up the cameras. The location we settled on at the last minute was a private parking lot in Santa Monica, which worked out well.

Because we sometimes filmed more than one episode at a location, or produced an episode using footage from various sites, the photos are presented on the following pages by location rather than by episode.

Santa Monica Mountains

Preparing for the first shoot. When we scouted this site the previous week, it was freezing. However, the day of the shoot it was hot. Very hot. We were swarmed by tiny flies who delighted in flying into mouths and noses. Our initial budget was very tight and didn't allow us the luxury of a large screen to blot out the bright sunlight. We therefore ended up not using most of the footage because Kirk and Ray were squinting under the painful glare of reflectors. At the end of the day they were both so sunburned, they looked like tomato heads.

The scenic Santa Monica Mountains. The scenes shot here were used in later episode

VIEWER'S QUESTION

"How many people are needed for filming?"

We usually film with a crew of about a dozen people. This includes a hired lighting crew (two or three people), two camera operators, the director, sound engineer, on-set photographer, a couple of "grips" to help carry equipment, and a script supervisor (to make sure nothing is omitted) . . . plus Kirk and Ray. Depending on the location, we may have to employ a policeman, fireman, or park ranger to be on the set during the whole shoot. It's best to keep on-set visitors to a minimum, because it is easy for the person on camera to be distracted during filming when others whisper, laugh, cough, or sneeze, or even move their head. When the camera is rolling, the slightest disturbance can ruin a scene.

Ray playing "director."

WORDS OF COMFORT

WE THOUGHT IT was important to begin the series by establishing the evangelistic responsibility of the Church. If we didn't, some may just watch the program for its entertainment value and carry on, involved in the usual Christian activities, without seeking the lost. The Bible uses firefighters as an analogy for the urgent nature of the Christian's responsibility, so that's what we decided to do. This was even more relevant in light of the valiant work of firefighters in the tragedy of 9/11. My original thought was to have Kirk read this from a news desk in a studio, but we eventually decided to do it as a location report.

The opening scene for the first "The Way of the Master" episode, "The Firefighter."

Here is the original script (note that the firefighter story is fictitious):

Episode #1: The Firefighter

An experienced New York[1] firefighter has just been charged with grave neglect of duty. Prosecutors maintained that he abandoned his responsibility and betrayed the people of New York when he failed to release rescue equipment at the scene of a fire. This resulted in the needless and tragic deaths of a family of five.

Eyewitnesses were sickened when they discovered that the reason the firefighter remained in the locked emergency vehicle was simply to test a new high-tech CD player, which he maintained that he had purchased as a gift for the fire chief.

The fire chief immediately distanced himself from the defendant, and dishonorably discharged him from the department. In a prepared statement he said that there were no words to describe such a betrayal of those he was sworn to protect.

The lead prosecuting attorney argued that for more than three minutes after arriving at the scene, the firefighter wore earphones and listened to a CD while a family of five screamed to be rescued from the sixth floor of a building. Horrified bystanders related that, as flames licked her clothing, a mother cried out in terror and fell to her death while still clutching an infant in her arms.

The distraught onlookers also said that the father held onto two terrified children as he was engulfed by the massive flames. This terrifying drama took place in full view of the firefighter as he remained seated in the vehicle listening to the CD.

The defense pleaded "no contest," but added that the defendant had gone to great personal sacrifice to purchase the expensive gift for the chief, and that he hoped the judge would take that into account when passing sentence.

What do you think is a fitting punishment for this serious crime? Should he receive a strong reprimand, two years in prison, twenty years, a life sentence, or perhaps capital punishment?

Do you enjoy worshiping God? Most of the modern Church does. All across the country auditoriums are full of hand-raising, God-loving Christians. That's understand-

(continued)

[1] *The words "New York" were later removed out of respect for the valiant firefighters who lost their lives on 9/11.*

able, because when the Holy Spirit dwells within the believer it's not hard to worship our glorious and worthy Creator.

It is as natural for the godly to worship the Lord as it is for flowers to open in the warmth of sunlight. The sunshine of His great love opens the sweet-smelling petals of praise. Yet, the "sacrifice of praise" isn't so great a sacrifice in light of the sacrifice of the cross.

Rather, our love for Him is more evidenced by our obedience to do His will, and that doesn't come so naturally. It takes a concerted effort to obey the Great Commission and follow in the footsteps of Jesus to seek the lost. Our professed love and worship of God should evidence a determined devotion to do His will.

The photographer, Carol Scott, takes a break.

When then did you last do His will and share your faith with an unsaved person? When did you last meditate on the fact that all who die in their sins will be cast into the Lake of Fire? In his book *The Coming Revival*, Dr. Bill Bright stated that only 2 percent of the American Church regularly share their faith with others. Most are so locked into worship (with the volume turned high) that they have little or no thought for the fate of the ungodly.

If you and I are not seeking to "save [the lost] with fear, pulling them out of the fire, hating even the garment defiled by the flesh" (Jude 23), then we are the firefighter. If we call Jesus "Lord," but refuse to do the things He has commanded us to do, then He is not our "Lord," and He will distance Himself from us on the Day of Judgment, despite our professed sacrifice of praise. When we cry out, "Lord, Lord!" He will say, "Depart from me . . . I never knew you."

What sentence did you give the New York firefighter? Are you honest enough to judge yourself by the same standard? Think of the terrifying fate of that poor family. Think of his dreadful neglect of duty. He was no firefighter. He was a Judas . . . a contemptible traitor. Their blood was on his hands.

Now, think of the terrible fate of the lost. They will be cast into a Lake of Fire. Think of your neglect of duty. Is Jesus your Lord? What then will be your defense if you do nothing to reach the lost, on the Day that you stand before His Judgment throne (2 Corinthians 5:10)?

Charles Spurgeon said, "Have you no wish for others to be saved? Then you are not saved yourself. Be sure of that."

Oswald J. Smith said, "Oh my friends we are loaded down with countless church activities, while the real work of the Church, that of evangelizing and winning the lost is almost entirely neglected." We have been gazing to the heavens while sinners are sinking into Hell.

Worship is the highest calling of the Christian, and we can see in the Book of Revelation that in the future the Church will one day be consumed in worship before the Throne of the Almighty. But when we look back at the Book of Acts, we don't find that the Church was consumed with worship. Instead we find that they were devoted to reaching the lost, to a point where they willingly gave their lives to preach the gospel.

Los Angeles Warehouse

The exterior of the run-down Los Angeles warehouse used for the teaching of "The Firefighter" episode.

A time of prayer before beginning a shoot in the old Los Angeles warehouse. We never took anything for granted, but prayed before shoots, asking God to give us wisdom and bless our efforts.

Making a point during the teaching.

Mark Spence, Dean of the online School of Biblical Evangelism, joins the crew for the teaching of "The Firefighter" episode.

The camera's-eye view.

WORDS OF COMFORT

DUANE HAD SUCH a good eye when it came to locations. He knew what worked and what didn't. I would never have chosen an old warehouse in downtown Los Angeles. But it looked great on camera.

A little "tongue-in-cheek" during makeup.

Filming a "filler," a short segment to drop in-between the main scenes of each show. Pictured are Duane Barnhart on camera, Stuart ("Scotty") Scott and Ron Meade on sound, Emeal ("EZ") Zwayne with a reflector board, and Kirk watching.

Sharing our food with homeless families.

Praise & worship after a long day's shoot.

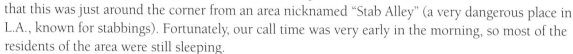

"STAB ALLEY" — KIRK CAMERON

THIS SHOOT took place in downtown Los Angeles. I drove through one of the worst parts of the city that I had ever seen. The streets were lined with hundreds of homeless people living in tents and makeshift plastic huts. I later learned that this was just around the corner from an area nicknamed "Stab Alley" (a very dangerous place in L.A., known for stabbings). Fortunately, our call time was very early in the morning, so most of the residents of the area were still sleeping.

We shot in an upper room of a 100-year-old warehouse used to process wiping materials from discarded shirts, trousers, and blankets. Our set was a wonderfully weathered, old brick room—perfect for our first episode, entitled "The Firefighter: The Case for Evangelism."

This episode was so important because it was the "pilot" for the series and it was used to represent our vision to the TV networks, at the Christian Booksellers Association (CBA) Convention, and to all potentially interested partners. It seemed par for the course to have the electric company fixing a power line just outside our windows, working on a crane lift that emitted that "beeping" sound each time we rolled our cameras, making it impossible to get our shots done. We were off to a late start and had the room for only nine hours, so we had to make up time by doing fewer takes.

With a laptop computer and a slide projector, we had flames as part of our backdrop while we spoke about how we, as Christians, are like firefighters who rescue people from burning buildings. We must take no thought for ourselves when it comes to seeking the lost, "[saving them] with fear, pulling them from the fire, hating even the garments spotted by the flesh" (Jude 23). What a sobering message this was. We also filmed two more episodes here, titled "Theft" and "Lie & Covet." We had our work cut out for us, but with God's help, we did it.

During a much needed break, Ray lifted a box of bottled water off of a table (which was balancing fruit, granola bars, chips, etc.), causing the entire table to flip up into the air, spilling everything onto the floor. Instead of getting upset, everyone just laughed, because they knew this was very normal for this New Zealand kiwi. In fact, his book *Comfort, the Feeble-Minded* documents all the ridiculous mishaps that have occurred in the world due to Ray Comfort being around. He is chronically clumsy and things like this always seem to happen whenever he is nearby. So, if you happen to see Ray Comfort walking down the street, hold on to your chips and run in the opposite direction!

We brought in Burger King fast food for lunch and took some burgers, fries, and drinks to the homeless families living in the tent village behind our warehouse. They were grateful. We finished up our work for the day, completed all three episodes, and went home. What a blessing to be working on a program that could impact millions for the Kingdom.

Pepperdine University

Pepperdine University in Malibu kindly allowed us to film in their beautiful chapel, where we shot several of the initial episodes.

Duane holds the attention of Kirk and the crew over lunch.

Witnessing to a member of the lighting crew (below). We should never take for granted that people are saved simply because they are sympathetic to the message. We hired lighting crews who were very congenial and even apprecia- tive of what is being taught in the episode, so it was easy to presume they knew the Lord and excuse ourselves of the irksome task of witnessing to them. But love cannot take the easy path when someone's eternal destiny may be at stake.

A simple and inoffensive way to probe a person's soul is to ask if he thinks he is a good person. A false convert or someone who doesn't know the Lord will almost always claim to be a morally good person. That's why we must learn the way of the Master and, with the help of God, slay what Martin Luther called "the beast of self-righteousness."

If sinners be damned, at least let them leap to Hell over our bodies. If they will perish, let them perish with our arms about their knees.
—CHARLES SPURGEON

We had only a certain amount of time to shoot so Kirk said, "Let's do a role-play." The role-play segment was hardly rehearsed and yet it turned out to be one of the best examples of how to witness to a friend or stranger.

The director directs.

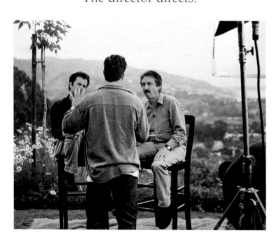

Teaching an episode called "David and Bathsheba." This was never used for technical reasons.

A quick call to our wives, between shoots.

Before leaving for Pepperdine, we preached at the local court (something we do every week day), then gave free books to those who wanted them. Within one hundred feet of the ministry, 40 to 70 people, from all walks of life, line up to see the judge for misdemeanor crimes.

As funds became available, we were able to afford sun shields and light diffusers.

Hollywood

Kirk goes through his lines on the balcony (out in the fresh air) as we prepare to shoot in what we called "the dirty little Hollywood hotel."

WORDS OF COMFORT

HOLLYWOOD IS ONLY about a 30-minute drive from our production studio. That's if the Los Angeles traffic is okay. If traffic is bad, Hollywood is about three days from the studio. Duane had connections in a hotel in Hollywood that he said had a lot of character. It did. But when we turned our camera lights on, it looked as though it hadn't been cleaned since the early 1700s. Adding to the dusty atmosphere of the hotel was the fact that tenants were allowed to have dogs in their rooms. Murphy's law made sure that as soon as we started filming, every man and his dog would walk through the lobby growling and snorting. The dogs were noisy too.

Hollywood Blvd. The use of the "boom" microphone had the advantage of being out of the shot, but it sometimes attracted authorities whose job it was to hassle film crews.

VIEWER'S QUESTION

"Kirk, do you find that being a celebrity ("Growing Pains," *Left Behind*, etc.) is a help or a hindrance when it comes to sharing your faith with strangers?"

Let me (Ray) answer this for Kirk, because I have seen him witness to many people. It can be both a blessing and a curse. His celebrity gives him instant acceptance with almost everyone. That's the blessing part. However, we have hours of videotape of google-eyed females who are passively agreeing with everything Kirk is telling them, but they are not taking it to heart. They are saying, "Yes, I'm going to Hell . . . May I have your autograph?" That can be very frustrating for him.

A continual problem Kirk had when sharing the gospel with "Growing Pains" fans was that they were awed by his celebrity and, for awhile, hardly listened to a thing he said.

Kirk interviews a Hindu doctor.

This was a very special interview. This man was self-righteous, but as soon as he heard the Commandments, he not only admitted his guilt, but he understood the cross. He kept saying things like, "I comprehend what you are saying… This has been a wake-up call."

WORDS OF COMFORT

THE PURPOSE OF the Ten Commandments is to give us a wake-up call. They wake up a sleeping sinner to his true state before God. Perhaps you are familiar with Acts 12, where Peter was arrested by King Herod and put in prison, to be executed the following day. Peter lay soundly asleep that night in Herod's prison. He was bound with chains between two soldiers, and more guards stood at the door of the prison. Suddenly an angel of the Lord appeared and stood by him, "and a light shined in the prison." It is strongly implied that the light didn't awaken Peter, because the Scriptures then tell us that the angel struck him on the side. As he arose, his chains fell off, he clothed himself, tied on his shoes, put on his garment, and followed the angel. The iron gate leading to the city then opened of its own accord, and Peter was free.

The sinner is in the prison of his sins. He is captured by the devil, bound by the chains of sin and death. What's more, he's asleep in his sins. He lives in a dream world. But it isn't the gospel light that will awaken him. How can "Good News" alarm a sinner? Rather, the Law must strike him. He needs to be struck with the Commandments and awakened by their thunderings. That will show him his danger—he is on the brink of death and Hell.

Then he will arise and the light of the gospel will remove the chains of sin and death. It will be "the power of God to salvation." He will clothe himself with truth, tie on his gospel shoes, put on the garment of righteousness, follow the Lord, and the iron gate of the Heavenly City will open to him.

VIEWER LETTER

4 a.m. wake-up call

I just wanted to tell you that "The Way of the Master" is phenomenal. I am feeling much more equipped to share my faith without intimidation. Last Saturday morning at 4:00 a.m. the Lord awakened me with an urgency to go and share with my mother-in-law. She was raised Mormon but now attends a Methodist church because she says she prefers 1 hour sermons to their 3 hours.

I called her that morning and went over to visit. When she started talking about her family wanting her to come back to the Mormon church, I asked her if she thinks about eternal things. She replied yes and I asked her if she died tonight, did she think she would go to heaven? When she said she hoped so, it was a perfect opening for me to say, "Would you like to take a test to find out?" I then led her through the "good person" test using the Law. She decided she was headed for hell with all of her friends and she laughingly said she wasn't concerned. When I described what the Bible says hell is like, her lip began to quiver, then I shared with her about Jesus and what God had done for her because He loves her. We prayed together and she received Jesus. She was weeping and thanking me for coming over and talking to her. She hugged me tight for a long time and later when I went to leave, she started weeping again out of gratefulness. She was a different woman when I left.

You are right—people will thank you! I am praising God for that awesome privilege and also for your program, and for your boldness to do this. I am praying for you and this ministry. This is long overdue—keep on preaching the truth!

—Sherry P., Arizona

VIEWER'S QUESTION

"How long on average does it take to film each segment?"

It could take up to 8–10 hours just to get 15 minutes of film for the teaching part of each episode. This is because of needed retakes, or because of car noises, passing planes, barking dogs, jackhammers, lawn mowers, etc. There were also continual lighting, wind, and other sound problems. We were always very prayerful as we began a shoot because we knew that many interruptions were spiritual by nature.

A huge mural inside a Hollywood parking garage made an interesting backdrop.

All God's giants have been weak men who did great things for God because they reckoned on His being with them.
—HUDSON TAYLOR

Here's looking at you, kid.

Kirk commentates "live" with a hidden camera, while Ray witnesses to three young men at the Third Street Promenade in Santa Monica. This segment was used in episode one.

"Groucho Marx" makes a point in front of the famous Grauman's Chinese Theatre on Hollywood Blvd.

A light moment between Duane and Kirk, while Minneapolis radio talk show host Todd Friel prepares to record for his program.

Todd Friel interviews for his radio program, "Talk the Walk."

Sharing the gospel with a cigar-smoking young lady while a hidden camera recorded the interview. Sadly, she refused to give permission for the footage to be used.

This interview was used in the "Conscience" episode.

VIEWER'S QUESTION

"Do you have to get permission to interview people?"

We live in an age of litigation, so we have to be careful that we always get permission to use footage of individuals. If we take people through the Law but they haven't given us permission to use the interview, they could sue us claiming that they were humiliated on camera (when they were simply humbled). It takes boldness to obtain "sign offs" because you have to approach complete strangers and ask, "Would you like to be interviewed for TV?" Most people say no and walk away, leaving you feeling as though you were trying to sell them something. Others may stop and ask for details.

The sign-off sheet is a full page of legalese. We found that if we said something like, "This gives us the legal right to use your image for television," the person would feel embarrassed not to read the whole thing before signing it. But if we said, "It gives us the right to your house, your car, your firstborn, and your income for the next twenty years . . . and it gives us the right to use your face," they would laugh and sign it without hesitation.

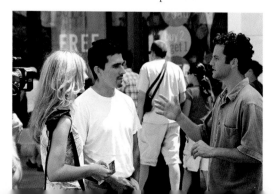

Kirk and Todd witnessing.

Santa Monica Pier.

The Ten Commandments are like ten great cannons pointing at sinful humanity.

I would not have known what sin was except through the law.
—ROMANS 7:7

WORDS OF COMFORT

WE WERE INTERVIEWING different people on Santa Monica Pier when Kirk spotted a Mexican gang walking by. He grabbed a cameraman and told him to start the camera rolling. By the time Duane added sound effects, the sequence ended up being the most exciting of the entire series, as Kirk took hardened gang members through the Law into the cross. It was a graphic example of how we can speak the truth in love, and when the conscience is addressed, there is no offense. These men had no idea who Kirk was (so they weren't aware of his celebrity), and they sincerely thanked him for taking the time to speak to them about the things of God.

Witnessing to gang members at the Santa Monica Pier.

Yorba Linda

We were very fortunate to be able to film a number of episodes at the beautiful home of the Peiffers in Yorba Linda. This house looked like something out of a fairy tale.

The cameras are positioned together so that we can match "tight" (close-up) and "wide" (faraway) shots with a filter over the lights to even out the lighting—to cut down the glare.

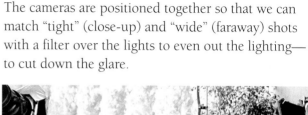

VIEWER'S QUESTION

"Were there any humorous events that happened during the filming?"

EZ, General Manager of "The Way of the Master," observes while Kirk and Ray go through the script.

Although we all realized that we had a serious mission, the filming of each episode was thoroughly lubricated with the oil of joy. There was always a lot of laughter on the set.

A "heart-felt" moment.

HOW EPISODES ARE PRODUCED
— RAY COMFORT

Setting up for the episode on the conscience.

This beautiful Hollywood house was loaned to us for the episode.

EACH PROGRAM begins with an idea, often from an existing teaching, such as "Atheism" or "How to Get on Fire for God." If Kirk likes the idea, we meet with Duane and EZ for a "pre-production" meeting. We then find an appropriate location (for example, we chose a beautiful lake for "Atheism" because it showed God's handiwork), and we apply for permits, book the various production crews, and secure insurance, travel, and all other necessary arrangements. We eventually arrive on location, do the taping, and then I am entrusted with the raw footage. This always makes me nervous because I am so aware that all our hard work is in my possession, and if I lose it we have to start from scratch.

Back at the ministry, Ron in the Production Department edits all the raw footage together to make a rough program. This is complex, as each scene has multiple takes, as well as two camera angles (one close-up and one wide angle). Once that is done, Duane meets with Dale in our Graphics Department to give direction to the graphic look for that particular episode. Meanwhile, I have a large computer file in which I have logged each individual "on-the-street" witnessing clip that we have recorded over the years. This contains hundreds of hours of interviews with people from all over the world. I have created another file indicating what I consider to be the most interesting and equipping encounters with some of the most colorful people we've ever met. I give these shots to Ron, and he captures all the interviews together and files them on our computer network where the producer can access them. Duane inserts the interviews where we think is the best placement and does his magic with the final edits, including sound, transitions, fades, etc. Duane has inherited the artistic gifts of his father (a professional lyricist for Sony Music with several #1 hit songs to his credit), and he can make a mundane scene electric simply by adding suitable sound.

Kirk is sent a master DVD, which he studies closely and makes notes about how he thinks the episode can be improved. He comes to the ministry's editing suite with his notes in hand, the three of us pray, and then spend hours methodically going through the episode, moving interviews, deleting scenes, and adding graphics. By the end of the day we are usually delighted and amazed with what has come together. Many times we marvel that we are allowed by God to be involved in such an exciting and important ministry, and humbly thank Him for such an honor.

The interior decor of this
Hollywood home was exquisite.

Answering God's call
to evangelism.

THE CONSCIENCE SCRIPT

The contents of the scripts would almost always change during filming, to make a point clearer or to develop another important thought.

RAY: Previous programs.

KIRK: The dictionary tells us that the conscience is "the human faculty that enables one to decide between right and wrong acts or behavior, esp. in regard to one's own conduct." It is that impartial judge in the courtroom of the mind.

RAY: Stealing an eraser.

KIRK: Fire crackers...able to silence my conscience (dove under the car).

Bring in the Law, they will flee from the wrath to come. What Adam did in the garden and what man has been doing ever since—running from God.

RAY: The Bible says that God has given "light" to every man. God has given every man and woman a conscience—primitives, etc. The word "conscience" means "with knowledge." Whenever we sin, we do so "with knowledge."

KIRK: How do we use the conscience to reach the lost? By taking a person through the Commandments like Jesus did in Mark 10, Luke 18, Luke 10, etc.

Computer chip analogy. When you go into your room and close the door.

FILLER: Seared—Hawaii chef.

RAY: Sophisticated calculator. Recorded. 20 years. Music. Smell. Stirs up memory. God will access all those records on the Day of Judgment.

INSERT CLIPS FROM WDJD.

KIRK: Here's a tragic thing. Modern evangelism actually *avoids* going where we should be going—it doesn't want to make the sinner feel guilty. It doesn't want to cause any offense. But guilt isn't a bad thing, because it leads us to the door of mercy...of seeking God's forgiveness. It leaves in the "All have sinned" message, but that doesn't probe the conscience. It spreads sin and generalizes it, instead of making it personal. We need to remind sinners of their personal sins, and that there are two witnesses to their crimes against God—their conscience and God.

RAY: Your little boy cuts his leg on a rusty piece of tin...

KIRK: Charles Spurgeon said in this regard to those who are more concerned about their own fear of rejection than the eternal welfare of the lost: "Ho, ho sir surgeon, you are too delicate to tell the man that he is ill! You hope to heal the sick without their knowing it. You therefore flatter them; and what happens? They laugh at you; they dance upon their own graves. At last they die! Your delicacy is cruelty; your flatteries are poisons; *you are a murderer.* Shall we keep men in a fool's paradise? Shall we lull them into soft slumbers from which they will awake in hell? Are we to become helpers of their damnation by our smooth speeches? In the name of God we will not."

RAY: If we water down medicine it reduces its curative properties. It may taste palatable to the sinner, but it doesn't help him. When we leave out any mention of the Law and the personal nature of sin, we leave the conscience dormant. Think of the woman caught in adultery—"being convicted in their conscience." What did Jesus write in the sand? Why in the sand? Law written in stone. But with Jesus, removable—seat of God's mercy.

RAY (FILLER): Dentist probes and you feel pain, convinces to let him drill and fill. Probe with Law.

KIRK: Drunk comes into a dark room and thinks he sees two candles. Many snuff out the light and abandon themselves to the dark world of sin, not realizing the terrible consequences of their actions. Look at what A. W. Tozer said about how readily idolatry is embraced by a dulled conscience: "God's justice stands forever against the sinner in utter severity. The vague and tenuous hope that God is too kind to punish the ungodly has become a deadly opiate for the consciences of millions. It hushes their fears and allows them to practice all pleasant forms of iniquity while death draws every day nearer and the command to repent goes unregarded. As responsible moral beings, we dare not so trifle with our eternal future." —A. W. Tozer, *The Knowledge of the Holy*

FILLER: Batteries in the smoke detector.

FILLER (done): Dog and drunk.

CLIPS

REMEMBER TO CHIT CHAT

KIRK: To the world, the conscience is a "party pooper." Think about it. If you're about to sleep with your girlfriend or boyfriend, the last thing you want to hear is the voice of your conscience. It spoils the fun. It's as bad as having your mother watching your every move. Our conscience reminds us of God. His moral standards are linked via DSL to it. It is called "the work of the Law." That means it is the "outworkings" of the Law. So people have practiced ignoring their conscience, putting it to sleep. What we need to do is wake it up and let it speak to the sinner. Look at these wise words from Spurgeon, the Prince of Preachers:

"When once God the Holy Spirit applies the Law to the conscience, secret sins are dragged to light, little sins are magnified to their true size, and things apparently harmless become exceedingly sinful. Before that dread searcher of the hearts and trier of the reins makes His entrance into the soul, it appears righteous, just, lovely, and holy; but when He reveals the hidden evils, the scene is changed. Offenses which were once styled peccadilloes, trifles, freaks of youth, follies, indulgences, little slips, etc., then appear in their true color, as breaches of the Law of God, deserving condign punishment."

CLIPS

RAY: Remember that the human mind is at enmity with God. It's not subject to the Law of God. There is a war between the mind and God. We are "enemies of God in our minds" until we make peace with Him. And never forget the ally in the heart of the enemy—the sinner's conscience. It will not fight against you. Instead it will work with you. It is independent of his sin-loving will. Sin, however, has the conscience tied hand and foot and its voice gagged. You have to cut the ropes with the sharp edge of the sword of God's Law and untie the gag. Don't be afraid to say things like, "God gave you a conscience. You know right from wrong. Listen to the voice of your conscience—it will remind you of sins that you have committed." It will encourage you in battle when you hear its voice coming through. It is the work of the Law written on their hearts. It will bear witness with the Law of God (see Romans 2:15).

CLIPS

The seared conscience is like a seared steak—hardened on the outside.

Fellowship with two young helpers.

It is the ordinary method of the Spirit of God to convict sinners by the Law. It is this which, being set home on the conscience, generally breaketh the rocks in pieces. It is more especially this part of the Word of God which is quick and powerful, full of life and energy and sharper than any two-edged sword.
—JOHN WESLEY

Spirit West Coast

Showing the incredible
Curved Illusion tract.

The Million Dolla
Bill tract.

An estimated 20,000 people listen to
Ray preach "Hell's Best Kept Secret."

A quick conference before Kirk shares
with a crowd that was bursting at the
seams. The event organizers had never
seen such an overwhelming response
to any speaker.

Darren Streblow, a friend and
stand-up Christian comedian.

Duane takes a fall
while messing
around between
filming interviews.

One of our favorite interviews: "Do you talk about sin when you share your faith?" "Sin? You mean . . . talk about it?" So many Christians are afraid to mention the word "sin" when it comes to sharing their faith, but without mentioning sin, the cross makes no sense.

Ray strikes a humorous chord while being interviewed about the ministry by a local TV show that was covering the event. They filmed us and we took pictures of them.

Cool dude.

This interview really stood out above the rest.

VIEWER'S QUESTION

"Are the show's production costs high?"

Most people don't realize how much it costs to produce an episode. The expense isn't just for cameras, wages, airfare, hotel costs, and the lighting crew. There are always hidden extras, such as permits, special fees, and insurance. We need special insurance in case some lawyer calls and says, "My client's son was watching your program. When he realized that he was a liar and a thief, he went out and shot himself. We will see you in court."

The world's pleasures and the world's treasures henceforth have no appeal for me. I reckon myself crucified to the world and the world crucified to me. But the multitudes that were so dear to Christ shall not be less dear to me. If I cannot prevent their moral suicide, I shall at least baptize them with my human tears.

I want no blessing that I cannot share. I seek no spirituality that I must win at the cost of forgetting that men and women are lost and without hope. If in spite of all I can do they will sin against light and bring upon themselves the displeasure of a holy God, then I must not let them go their sad way unwept.

I scorn a happiness that I must purchase with ignorance. I reject a heaven that I must enter by shutting my eyes to the sufferings of my fellow men. I choose a broken heart rather than any happiness that ignores the tragedy of human life and human death.

Though I, through the grace of God in Christ, no longer lie under Adam's sin, I would still feel a bond of compassion for all of Adam's tragic race, and I am determined that I shall go down to the grave or up into God's heaven mourning for the lost and the perishing.

—A. W. TOZER

Santa Monica

Reviewing the day's proposed shoot at Santa Monica.

Crowds flock to Santa Monica Beach to cool down.

A golden mermaid sits on the pier.

We were able to do a few interviews before the police spotted the cameras and moved us off the pier.

Duane witnesses off camera.

VIEWER'S QUESTION

"How do people you witness to usually respond after their interview?"

When we take people through the Commandments into grace, it's common, once the camera is turned off, for them to say something like, "That was very interesting. I *really* appreciated what you said." Unfortunately, when the camera is turned back on for them to repeat what they said, it never has the genuineness and spontaneity of the first time. So we would often keep the cameras rolling after an interview to try to capture candid moments.

Ashley Lee interviews a woman on the Third Street Promenade.

Ashley has a tough interview with a hardened skeptic.

Some fans.

WORDS OF COMFORT

HOW DO YOU speak to someone who doesn't believe the Bible? Simple—don't mention the Bible. Instead, speak directly to his conscience. Ask him if he thinks he is a good person, and then take him through the Ten Commandments. Say something like the following:

Have you ever told a lie? This includes any fibs, white lies, half-truths, or exaggerations told in the past. Remember, time doesn't forgive sin. God sees the sins of your youth as though they were committed yesterday. If you have told even one lie, then you are a liar (be brutally honest with yourself, because God will be on the Day of Judgment). Don't pull back from the mirror just because you detect a blemish. Stay close so that you can see yourself clearly.

Have you ever stolen something? The value of the item is totally irrelevant. If you have stolen one thing, then you are a thief. Have you committed murder, or have you desired to by harboring hatred in your heart? If you have hated someone, the Scriptures say that you are a murderer. Jesus said, "Whoever looks upon a woman to lust after her has committed adultery already with her in his heart." Have you ever looked at someone with lust? Have you had sex outside of marriage, or committed adultery, or desired to? Then you have committed sexual sin and cannot enter Heaven.

Have you kept the Sabbath holy, always honored your parents, always put God first in your affections, loving Him with all of your heart, soul, mind, and strength? Have you always loved your neighbor as much as you love yourself? Most of us have trouble loving our "loved ones," let alone loving our neighbors. Have you ever used God's holy name in vain, either employing it as a filthy curse word, or failing to give it due honor? Have you made a god to suit yourself and therefore been guilty of "idolatry"—making a god in your own image, believing in your version of what you think God is like? Have you ever desired anything that belonged to someone else?

If you have broken even one of these Ten Commandments, then you have sinned against God. On Judgment Day every sin you have ever committed will come out as evidence of your guilt. God sees your unclean sexual thoughts, those imaginations you enjoyed, which you thought no one knew about. He has seen the things you have done in darkness, the lies, the stealing, the gossip, the failure to do what's right. Nothing is hidden from His holy, pure eyes.

If all those thoughts, deeds, and words come out as evidence on that Day, you will be damned forever, and lose your soul. Without God's mercy, you will go to Hell. Such a thought horrifies me. Please don't let that happen to you. Listen to your conscience, that impartial judge in the courtroom of your mind. Don't muffle its voice. What is your conscience saying

(continued)

Larry Lee conducts interviews on the Promenade.

Larry and Ashley Lee discuss some important issues about evangelism with Kirk.

(continued)

to you? Is it agreeing with God's Law? Is it doing its God-given duty? I certainly hope so.

Don't add self-righteousness to your sins by saying that you are basically a "good" person. If you refuse to admit that you are guilty, you will never seek God's mercy. Don't think that He will overlook your sins because He is good. His "goodness" will ensure that justice is done. As a just judge, He must punish all liars, thieves, adulterers, etc.

Don't be fooled into thinking you can clean up your life. No "good" you do can wash away your sins—only God's mercy can do that. Do you think a judge would dismiss the case of a guilty criminal because he says he will clean up his life in the future? Of course he should clean up his life. In the meantime, if he has broken the law, he must be punished.

There are many people who say, "But I confess my sins to God. I tell Him I'm sorry," thinking that will be enough to grant them entrance into Heaven. If you have those thoughts, consider this. If you find yourself in court with a $50,000 fine, will a judge let you go simply because you say you're sorry and you won't commit the crime again? Of course not. But if someone pays your $50,000 fine, will you be free from the demands of the law? Of course you will. The judge could then say, "This fine has been paid. You're free to go."

God will not forgive you on the basis that you are sorry. Of course we should be sorry for sin—we have a conscience to tell us that adultery, rape, lust, murder, hatred, lying, stealing, etc., are wrong. And of course we shouldn't sin again. However, God will only release us from the demands of eternal justice on the basis that Someone paid our fine. Two thousand years ago, God came to this earth in human form to take the punishment for us. When Jesus suffered and died on the cross, He stepped into the courtroom and paid our fine for us. His suffering satisfied the Law that you and I violated.

Did you see the movie *The Passion of the Christ*? I did. The palms of my hands began to sweat. I went into hyperventilation during the crucifixion, it was so brutal. Violent scenes in a movie are usually over in a moment, but in *The Passion of the Christ*, it went on, and on, and on. While there was some "artistic license" taken in the movie, the brutality was based on what we are told actually happened to Jesus of Nazareth. It says that He was "marred more than any man." He was "bruised for our iniquities." Think about what God did for you. He satisfied the demands of the Law, then He cried out, "It is finished!" In other words, the debt has been paid. Then He rose from the dead, defeating death forever. The moment we repent and trust the Savior, God forgives our sins and grants us everlasting life.

An Olympic gold-medalist high-diving champion once suffered from insomnia. As he tossed and turned in bed, he began thinking about the success he had attained and the medals he had won. To his dismay he realized that his success had not achieved what he had hoped. The excitement of winning, the photographers, the medals, and the fame had given him some pleasure, but the fact that death was awaiting him left him with a sense of futility.

He rose from the bed and made his way to his diving pool. Because the moon was full, he didn't bother to turn the lights on as he climbed the high-diving board. The routine had become so commonplace that he could confidently walk that board in semi-darkness. At the end of the board, he prepared to dive. He placed his feet together, then pulled his arms up to a horizontal position. As his eyes caught a glimpse of his shadow on the far wall, all he could see was a perfect cross. His mind immediately raced back to something he had learned in his Sunday school days: "God demonstrates His own love toward us, in that while we were still sinners, Christ died for us." He suddenly felt unclean as he considered the Commandments he had broken. The sinless Son of God had come to pay the penalty for his sins. He whispered a verse he had memorized as a child: "For God so loved the world that He gave His only begotten Son, that whoever believes in Him should not perish but have everlasting life."

With tears in his eyes, the great athlete turned around, slowly made his way down to the bottom of the diving board, fell to his knees, and yielded his life to Jesus Christ. He was then able to go back to bed and sleep peacefully.

In the morning he arose with a new sense of forgiveness of his sins. He made his way back to the pool, but to his utter astonishment, *it was completely empty*. The previous evening, the caretaker had emptied it and was just beginning the process of refilling.

Imagine if he had said, "It's true. I am a sinner. I believe that Jesus died for me. *Tomorrow* I will get right with God . . . ," and then taken that dive.

What do you see when you look in the mirror of God's Law? If you see that you are unclean, then it's time for you to wash. If you care about your eternal salvation, don't put it off until tomorrow. Tomorrow may never come. Today, tell God that you are sorry for your sins, and then turn from them in humble repentance. Think of it this way—imagine you are a man who has committed adultery. You have violated the trust of a loving and faithful wife. She is willing to forgive you, so how can you reconcile the relationship? You humble yourself, tell her you are truly sorry. . . then vow to never commit adultery again. You shouldn't need someone to write words of sorrow for you to read to your wife, and you shouldn't have to read a prayer of repentance to God. Just pour yourself out to Him. It's your heart, not your words, that really matters. Then put your faith in Jesus as your Lord and Savior. Trust Him in the same way you would trust a pilot with your life when you fly. The pilot is merely a fallible man, so how much more should you trust in God? Then read the Bible daily and obey what you read, and God will never fail you.

Kirk gets behind the camera.

Anna Jackson, our supreme webmaster.

28

This was an interesting interview, but it couldn't be used because of sound problems.

Teens at a Quinceanera (fifteenth birthday party) receive Giant Money tracts.

Kirk uses a tract to witness to a former Mr. World titleholder.

Mr. World gives the Untearable Tract his best shot. (We won't tell you how he did.)

Talking with fans.

Ray interviews Mr. World.

Mr. World gives Ray a big hand.

This New Yorker was Jewish, and very colorful. She said that she didn't believe in the afterlife (she pronounced it "arferlyft"), and maintained that she was "a very good person." She ended up singing to the camera, much to Duane's amusement.

Rick Hart—a faithful laborer.

Luis Zepeda, Scotty, and Mark Spence.

WORDS OF COMFORT

WE RECEIVED A lot of email because of this interview. When this young lady realized that she had broken the Commandments she started weeping. Some of the email said that she had been horribly bullied, while others said that it was wonderful to see the Law do its work and bring a sinner to a point of contrition. When the first negative emails began coming in, we sat down and watched the sequence again to see if there was any merit in the negative criticism, and quickly came to the conclusion that there was no bullying on my part, but simply conviction of sin. The Law did the "bullying" and stirred her conscience to do its duty. No committed criminal is going to rejoice when he witnesses another criminal being arrested by the Law. Such a sight makes him feel threatened.

A girl begins to weep during an interview.

VIEWER LETTER

Hey man! I'm sick and tired of watching TBN to see you causing young girls to cry! Who the h-ll do you think you are? You were NOT appointed by God to point out other peoples sins! Work on your own self you hypocrite! You are self-righteous fundamentalists who thrive on making other people feel bad. Work on your OWN sins, and share the Gospel in love! You make women cry! I'm sick of it! That is NOT the right method. I am theologically and biblically educated, and your pharisaical (self-righteous) method is NOT biblical! Everyone I know cannot stand your cr-ppy show! You push people too far! WORK ON YOUR OWN SINS, HYPOCRITE! —Al

WORDS OF COMFORT

I WAS DUE TO appear on TV one night with Kirk to promote the second season of "The Way of the Master," and found (at the last minute) that we were wearing similar outfits. He was already on his way to the studio, so I decided to visit Southern California's only "short man's" store. Sue was busy, so I asked my friend Darrel Rundus (who is 6'5") to come with me to help me buy something tasteful. I threatened him about making short jokes while in the store. That didn't stop him.

We quickly picked out a pair of black pants that fit perfectly. Then we found two coordinating shirts and a tie, and while I was there I also grabbed a pair of short man's shorts. The clothes were expensive because there is a shortage of outfits for the not-so-tall, but it would be worth it.

I rushed home to discover that I didn't have any black socks. I also found that I didn't have any black shoes. So I couldn't wear my black pants that night. Nor could I wear the new shirts, because when I tried one on, it was too tight around my neck.

I gave both shirts away, and when I did try on the short shorts, I found that they flared at the bottom and made me feel like I was wearing a miniskirt.

At least I had a nice pair of black pants, even if I don't wear my horrible shorts and didn't have any shirts to go with my new tie. A little later I found to my surprise that I already had some black pants in my closet.

Men, always take your wife with you if you go shopping for clothes.

Kirk goes through his lines before the green screen filming for the opening page of "The Way of the Master" website.

Duane checks the sequence of shots as Kirk practices.

Giving free books and tracts to the listeners.

Preaching open-air at the courts before filming.

Lake Arrowhead

Interview at Lake Arrowhead.

"Do you consider yourself a good dog?"

The law of the Lord is perfect, converting the soul." (Psalm 19:7)

This man began the interview as an atheist, then backslid as we talked. The sequence was used in the "Atheism" episode

This man was a Christian who didn't see the value of gospel tracts.

Ray takes a few moments late one evening to do some writing.

Hume Lake

We deliberately chose a picturesque scene of God's creation for the backdrop of the "Atheism" episode, but it was so beautiful that it appeared to be a picture postcard. So we were pleased when someone rowed a boat across the lake while we were shooting.

The soda can and the banana—a tongue-in-cheek proof of the existence of God.

Near-freezing conditions while rehearsing for the "Atheism" episode.

Witnessing to parking attendants before leaving for Hume Lake.

Kirk takes a few moments to chat with fans

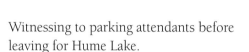

Kirk shows some tracts to Christians who were watching the filming.

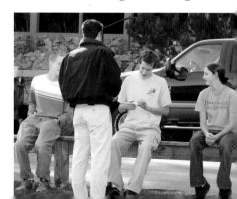

WORDS OF COMFORT

IT SHOULDN'T HAVE come as a shock to us that the enemy battled us every inch of the way with our TV program. Take, for instance, the shoot at Sequoia National Park. The week we were due to film, I developed a cough. It was no ordinary cough. Each attack was so violent I acquired washboard abs in just one day.

The same week, Ron, our cameraman, became so ill he said that every bone in his body ached. Kirk's kids got horribly sick and consequently his wife got no sleep. The day of the shoot, Scotty and Carol (our sound man and photographer) had to put their beloved dog to sleep, and both were in tears. Duane, our producer/director, had bronchitis so bad he could hardly breathe. The day before we left to film we learned that Sequoia National Park was at an 8,000-foot elevation, which Duane's doctor said would add to his breathing problems. The doctor was right. The night before the shoot, Duane was a mess. We prayed, and the next morning he was completely well.

Hume Lake Christian camp (which is in the Sequoia National Park) very kindly gave us permission to film on their property. After one program had been filmed, Kirk located a beautiful stream about two miles from the camp. We broke down our gear and relocated.

There were four stepping-stones in a scenic winding stream that were perfect for illustrating the four stepping-stones of sharing our faith. It was as though God had made the area for the program. As we were mapping out shots, there was a shout from above us. It was the park rangers. We were off private property and therefore needed a permit to shoot. We did have a permit to shoot in the "Sequoia

National Park," but this was "The Forest Service," which required a separate permit...and they wouldn't budge. Not an inch. They did, however, allow us to call their boss.

We drove back to the campground and put in a call to the Forest Service boss to plead with him to allow us to film. He couldn't be located, so one of the Hume Lake staff members mentioned that they had a stream on their property, and we were welcome to film there. Kirk, Duane, and I jumped onto an open golf cart and the man drove us to the location to scout it out.

As we turned onto a gravel road he mumbled, "Sorry about the dust." I looked behind me and saw both Kirk and Duane had their shirts pulled over their heads, and were gasping for breath in a huge cloud of fine dust stirred up from the road. I immediately thought of Duane and his bronchitis.

A few minutes later we arrived at the stream, and our Hume Lake guide apologized for its appearance. Since there had not been much rain lately, the stream was almost completely dried up. It looked like a drain. It was pathetic compared to the picturesque area in which we wanted to film. Things seemed hopeless. We would have to break down the gear again (which took time), and it was getting late in the day. We had hired a lighting crew, and they were due to leave at 5:00 p.m. We didn't even have an alternative shooting location.

It was ironic. God created and owned the stream, and we were forbidden from even filming it. We weren't exactly going to wear out the rocks. Besides, if we had been a group of guys who wanted to break out the booze and have a party at the stream, there wouldn't

have been a problem. Our clothes and shoes were now covered with dust. Kirk's dark hair looked gray with the fine dust. I was still coughing my little lungs out, and Duane could barely breathe. We decided to pray.

The three of us gathered together, and Duane asked God to move in our behalf, saying that the whole project was for His glory. It was a simple, earnest cry for help. Minutes later, we were told that the top man had been contacted, and he had given his okay for us to film. Pharaoh had let God's people film. What a blessing.

Other than a hired lighting man falling and breaking his wrist, and Ron getting altitude sickness the next day, we came through unscathed with two new programs. One, on the subject of atheism, was filmed in front of picturesque Hume Lake. The second program was unique. It was called "WDJD?" and was filmed at a beautiful little stream with four stepping-stones . . . thanks to God, and the top man at the Sequoia National Forest Service.

Duane frames the shot and Scotty checks sound while Kirk practices for the "WDJD?" episode.

*Ah, Lord GOD!
Behold, You have made the
heavens and the earth by Your
great power and outstretched
arm. There is nothing
too hard for You.*
—JEREMIAH 32:1

Kirk encourages viewers to share their faith with others.

"I'm ascared."

Capturing the final rays of sunlight with reflectors.

One of the larger examples of God's incredible creation.

AND THE DEAF WILL HEAR...

DURING THE TAPING of the "Atheist" episode at Hume Lake in Sequoia National Forest, I had a rather embarrassing moment.

We were set up on a large lawn in front of the lake and I couldn't believe how loudly every little sound carried. For me, the sound man, that was a nightmare. Every noise was magnified. Each time a car drove by, it seemed as though I could hear the tires roll over the pebbles on the road! So the volunteers with us began doing traffic control. We had to have a generator running for the lights, and I kept asking the lighting guys to move it further and further away because I could hear it so loudly. They eventually put it behind a truck 75 yards away. Guys held up wind breaks to lessen the wind noise and distant people talking were silenced. I was sensitive to every sound and was constantly complaining. Needless to say, I was a big pain. Finally it was as quiet as we could make it and we started shooting.

During filming, I keep my headphones over both ears and amplify the sound quite a bit. This way I can listen to what Kirk and Ray are saying and block out outside noise, but it also makes it difficult to hear when people are talking to me. We were in the middle of a scene when the filming suddenly stopped. As I looked around at Kirk and Ray, they were smirking and pointing in my direction. I thought they were pointing behind me. As I turned around I noticed others looking at me, some pointing and some saying something, but I couldn't hear them with the headphones on. I finally took my headphones off to find out what was wrong, and heard a strange beeping sound. I was still clueless until I heard, "Your watch! Your watch!" and realized my watch alarm had gone off and had been beeping all this time; and I, the sound man, was the only one on the set who didn't hear it! Boy, were the jokes flying.

—*Stuart ("Scotty") Scott*

Some of our helpers.

Posing with some fans.

UCLA

EZ preaches at the courts across from our ministry before we leave for UCLA.

This student was a hardened atheist. In the face of all the beauty of creation, she still professed to believe that it all came together by accident.

A student at UCLA (below). While we were able to obtain some interesting interviews at universities, we found that they were not typical of the average person on the street. The Bible says that "knowledge puffs up," and it is certainly evident at contemporary prestigious learning institutions.

VIEWER'S QUESTION

"Do you normally just dive into the interview questions, or do you start out by chatting with people, relaxing them with humor before leading into the presentation?"

We were always aware that when individuals are thrust in front of a camera, it can be a little nerve-racking, so we usually took a moment to ask people for their name, where they're from, etc. This puts most people at ease . . . until we take them through the Moral Law.

Duane uses an invaluable "shoulder holster," not only to keep the camera steady, but also to stop an aching back which inevitably comes when trying to hold a camera steady for any length of time. Cameramen are unsung heroes. Most people aren't conscious that they exist, until there is unnecessary camera movement.

Monkey Business

Planning the shoot before the entrance of our "special guest."

Ray and Bambam meet for the first time.

The special guest arrives on the set.

Comparing the similarities of the hands of the primate and the human.

Comparing feet.

Bambam actually picks up a banana with his feet!

WORDS OF COMFORT

He eats our lunch.

AFTER KIRK AND I decided to use an orangutan as a guest on the TV show, I rented the animal and thought that it would be interesting to film the three of us having lunch while talking about the subject of evolution. Kirk had worked with animals before, but for me it was like a dream come true, even if it did last for only a day. For years I had wanted to have my own monkey. I pestered Sue continually. She said that we had three kids and that should satisfy me. She stated that monkeys were dirty creatures. I retorted that babies were dirty creatures—more than a thousand dirty diapers each year proved that. I told her that I would dress him in diapers and blue shorts, a red shirt, suspenders, and white sneakers, and take him when I go open-air preaching. It couldn't help but pull in a crowd. I would call him "Link" and tell the listeners that Link was no longer missing. Not only that, but I would teach him to give out tracts about evolution.

Fortunately for Sue, when I inquired about it I discovered that California had very strict laws against owning chimps. So it was a big deal for me to have an orangutan for the day. I was so looking forward to the lunch scene.

Lunch was a disaster. We had Bambam walk into the restaurant with us and sit down. Everything went well until lunch was served. I made the mistake of ordering an ordinary salad for the orangutan. Our salads had the trimmings of cheese and colorful diced tomato. His was plain, boring green lettuce. When he saw ours, he went ape and guzzled our food while we were filming.

Then he sucked the plates and the books that were on the table, and even put his head under the tablecloth. It was like having lunch with Dennis the Menace on steroids.

I tried to reason with him, but it was no good. He wouldn't sit still for a moment. We quickly came to the conclusion that no one would listen to a couple of boring human beings talk about evolution while an ape was eating their lunch. Bambam stole the scene.

After lunch, we filmed the "missing link" sequence, and then posed for some still shots. As we were standing on the sidewalk a police car cruised by. The trainer looked worried and asked me, "Do you have a permit to have him outdoors?" I replied, "Do we need one?" We did. So we quickly escorted Bambam away from the scene, over to his van. I looked back at the police vehicle and saw that it was following us. Then it pulled right beside us. My heart was thumping. The window slowly rolled down, and an officer looked me directly in the eye, and said, "Can we have our photo taken with the orangutan?"

Tired orangutan, frustrated humans. NIGHTMARE.

Restaurant set for the "Evolution" episode.

The local police pose with Bambam ...and are given a tract.

Friends share a banana.

Scotty gets a little lovin'.

Bambam's recommended
reading material.

Ray—the missing link?

The missing link—still missing.

New York City

We decided that the New York footage should open with a helicopter shot, but it was very windy and the ride was so bumpy that we used only a few seconds of the footage in the opening of "God Has a Wonderful Plan for Your Life."

A very cold crew.

A New York helper, Tiffany Gelpi.

Sound man and photographer team, "Scotty" and Carol Scott.

This interview with "P-Nasty" was one of the most colorful of the entire series.

Wintry but colorful New York City.

It was very sobering to arrive at Ground Zero and realize that 3,000 people had so tragically lost their lives there.

These are the famous steel bars that were found in the form of the cross, and erected on the site. Strangely, there has been little complaint about the presence of the cross being a mixture of Church and State.

These two young ladies were enthusiastic when asked if they ever told non-Christians that "God had a wonderful plan for their lives." This was being filmed at Ground Zero. When asked if they would mention a "wonderful plan" to a thousand people who they knew were going to die the next day, they admitted that they would have to change the message. Their reactions were a godsend for the "God Has a Wonderful Plan for Your Life" episode.

This man—complete with windshield wipers on his glasses—explained (in very colorful language) what he hated about the Catholic church. However, he was still a Roman Catholic who, by his own admission, regularly showed up at the Mass reeking of alcohol.

A New Yorker responds positively to the gospel message. A Catholic, he said he now saw his need to receive God's forgiveness and be born again.

Unless we see our shortcomings in the light of the Law and holiness of God, we do not see them as sin at all.
—J. I. PACKER

An officer of the law being confronted with God's Law.

One of the many characters at Ground Zero. He was giving away burned matches that resembled the Twin Towers.

New York City — Kirk Cameron

RAY AND MOST of the crew arrived unscathed in New York City on schedule. But Ron Meade, our cameraman, forgot to remove a birthday gift of a Leatherman tool from his pocket before going through the airport's X-ray machines and, as a result, was held back by security and missed his flight. He caught the next one and joined the gang in the Big Apple later that evening. I arrived at midnight the following day and found my way to our hotel near Times Square. I heard about the adventures I had missed the day before: there were great witnessing encounters on the streets, as well as a run-in with a group of very well-dressed men in a restaurant. Judging by the subtle clues—these grown men publicly kissed each other on the lips, traveled with their own priest, and were very defensive about the Catholic religion—we surmised they were probably part of "The Family." They were mildly amused when Ray gave them some Million Dollar Bill tracts, then they laughed and wished our group Merry Christmas. Whew! Everyone in our group was glad to make it out alive.

The first day's shoot was in a fire station in Jersey City, just opposite the Statue of Liberty. The cold and dreary day accentuated our breath as it puffed out of our mouths and noses like smoke from a steam engine—perfect for that day's episode, "How to Get on Fire for God." The firefighters were very friendly and let us shoot almost all day, even repositioning the fire engines for us with lights flashing just to make our set really exciting. For lunch, they even offered us some real firemen's chili (that's what gives firemen such thick hair on their chests).

Just after Scotty, our sound man, got out of our cab, we heard a driver angrily honk his horn and holler loudly, "That's right—smash your door into my car!" Carol (Scotty's wife) mumbled, "How embarrassing." But when Ray got out of the same door, he was amazed to see the driver laughing and holding one of our Million Dollar Bill tracts. Scotty had said, "Sorry about that. Perhaps this will make up for it."

(continued)

Kirk makes a point during the "How to Get on Fire for God" shoot (and he makes a face or two between takes).

The New Jersey firefighters who kindly allowed us to film at their station.

Ron, goofing around in the fire truck.

Darrel Rundus witnesses to the New Jersey fire chief.

Grand Central Station at Christmas time.

The tract had put the man in such a good mood that Ray was able to witness to him.

When the sun went down, our police escort moved us to the Jersey City pier, directly across from "Ground Zero"—the site of the attack on the World Trade Center. The night sky was clear, the lights of the famous NYC skyline were beautiful, and we were pumped with adrenaline. To keep our fingers and toes from freezing, we ate lots of hot pizza and drank hot chocolate and coffee throughout the night. Fortunately, a friend of the ministry named "Brother Charles" worked at the Hyatt Hotel (100 yards from where we were shooting), and provided us with a warm room where we could take refuge from the freezing cold wind coming off the water. He had been given an *Evidence Bible* in the Philippines, loved it, contacted our ministry and was amazed to find that we were filming in his backyard. This episode was titled "God Has a Wonderful Plan for Your Life" and, thanks to the Lord and the crew's hard work, it did turn out to be a truly wonderful episode.

The next morning we began at Grand Central Station, the heart of NYC, where thousands of people flow like blood through the veins of the subway system. That day's episode was about how to break the ice with strangers. We talked about the effective use of well-written, striking gospel tracts. If you've never been to Grand Central Station . . . go there. The crowds, the energy, the rush, and the sound of the trains are so unique they will be forever etched in your mind. After completing the episode, as we were on the train back to Times Square, Ray stood up, got everyone's attention, and shared a Christmas gospel message with the passengers. Another member of our team then freely gave away "Good Samaritan" gifts of $20 to anyone who wanted one! People were blown away.

Times Square is truly "Vanity Fair." *Huge* video screens spanning entire office buildings, lights, music, a sea of people crowding the streets . . . and there we were talking with complete strangers about their faith. We stopped people and asked if they'd like to answer some questions for our TV special. One of the questions we began the interviews with was, "So this Christmas, have you been good or bad—naughty or nice?" Most would say, "Good," which led us right into asking if they'd kept God's Ten Commandments. One of our volunteers named Warner spoke to a homeless man, bought him dinner at McDonald's, and talked to him for over an hour, which resulted in the man asking for a Bible. Warner gave him one. We also did some filming at Rockefeller Center next to the world-famous Christmas tree and ice-skating rink. The night was electric and we were all exhausted by the time we finished at midnight.

Some of the team attended David Wilkerson's church in Times Square, and then went to Central Park, preached open-air, and afterward recorded some more interviews for the program.

On top of it all, we got to witness to cab drivers, hotel employees, tourists, and locals. This was a great trip and made for three wonderful new episodes of "The Way of the Master."

Going over the script for the "Tracts" episode.

Holding a Million Dollar Bill for the "Tracts" episode.

The beautiful New York skyline, from the New Jersey side.

Empire State Building at twilight.

VIEWER LETTER

Not willing that any should perish

I pastor a small church and have been praying for my brother Jack ever since I have been saved (22 years ago). Ray Comfort's teaching bore fruit last Monday. Jack is now 80 years old. He has had two heart attacks and a quadruple bypass, plus assorted other surgeries.

The Lord opened the door (twice) that day and after going through the "Do you consider yourself to be a good person" routine, Jack admitted to his condition and I asked him what he intended to do about it. "Repent?" I replied that was part of it, then told him that if he broke the law, even though he repented, the judge would still be required to find him guilty. He looked deep in thought. I then told him a story something like this:

Jack, say you decided to rob a bank one day and got away with $500,000. After some remorse over what you had done, you decided to give the money back. When you faced the judge, however, he took into account the fact that you had returned the money, but still was required to find you guilty of bank robbery. He said he would impose the minimum penalty required by law: one year probation and a fine of $25,000. "I don't have $25,000," you replied in anguish. "Take him away, bailiff. The law is the law." Came a voice from the back of the courtroom: "Your honor, I have already paid Jack's fine." "Who are you?" asked the judge. "My name is Jesus Christ. I died on a cross in payment for his sins 2,000 years ago." "Case dismissed," said the judge. "Bailiff, let the prisoner go free."

Jack bowed his head and received the Lord as his Savior.

Ray and Kirk, thank God for your teaching and for an opportunity to present it. I had witnessed to Jack many times, and had almost given up hope, but God is not willing that any should perish, not even Jack.

—*Dick, Colorado*

The backdrop for the "God Has a Wonderful Plan" shoot.

To tell an unbeliever that God has a wonderful plan for his life can be seriously misleading…We cannot dismiss the fact that God hates sin and punishes sinners with eternal torment. How can we begin a gospel presentation by telling people on their way to hell that God has a wonderful plan for their lives?

—JOHN MACARTHUR

Times Square nightlife.

A Florida couple go through
the "Good Test."

New York stockbrokers in
Times Square.

Witnessing in Times Square.

A friendly Scottish couple
agree to be interviewed.

New York Jews read tracts.

A feisty conversation.

When preaching and private talk are not available, you need to have a tract ready…Get good striking tracts, or none at all. But a touching gospel tract may be the seed of eternal life. Therefore, do not go out without your tracts.
—CHARLES SPURGEON

View of the skyline from Central Park.

Central Park.

Darrel Rundus, giving away money to draw a crowd in Central Park.

Ron Meade

It wasn't long before a crowd gathered.

In open-air preaching, the most difficult part is drawing a crowd. Here we were competing with ice skaters across from us.

VIEWER'S QUESTION

"Do you have any footage of times when open-air preaching or witnessing didn't go well? It would be educational to see how it was handled."

Yes, we do have footage of several witnessing encounters that didn't go very well. These were used in the program called "When Things Go Wrong." We anticipated that this would be a question viewers had, so we produced this show to encourage you that when things go wrong, it's nothing out of the ordinary.

HE WHO HAS EARS TO HEAR—RAY COMFORT

I WAS COMING down the stairs at The Way of the Master ministry, and saw an elderly man walking toward the glass doors of the building. As he entered, I said, "Hello. Did you get one of these?" and handed him a Million Dollar Bill tract. I was aware that elderly people have trouble reading the gospel message on that tract because it's in small print, so I handed him a coin that has the gospel on it. As I did so I had the thought that this man would also have trouble reading the text on the coin. As he smiled and walked on, I noted that the top inch of his right ear had been chewed off.

In the early hours of the next day, my conscience was gnawing at me. I should have asked him if he had a Christian background and spoken to him personally. But I had chickened out. The righteous are supposed to be "bold as a lion," not a chicken. How true are the words of Charles Spurgeon, "We must school and train ourselves to deal personally with the unconverted. We must not excuse ourselves, but force ourselves to the irksome task until it becomes easy." Even after so many years, I'm not at that point where it is always "easy."

That morning as I waited to preach to those standing outside the local courthouse, I looked at the crowd of about 40 people. Near the back of the line stood Mr. Chewed-ear. God had given me another chance to speak to him.

I earnestly went through the Law, then into grace. As I spoke about the cross, he turned a deaf ear to what I was saying, and began speaking to the person next to him. I directed my voice toward him and loudly said, "Sir, what I am saying is very important. I would appreciate your listening to me." Surprisingly, he stopped speaking and began to listen. I was so pleased. That's all we ask—that people listen, even if they have half an ear to do so.

Duane Barnhart.

Riding to work.

Sue Comfort, Ray's wife, giving out tracts at the courthouse.

The rich Hollywood director role-play, from "God Has a Wonderful Plan for Your Life."

Directing the rich man's butler.

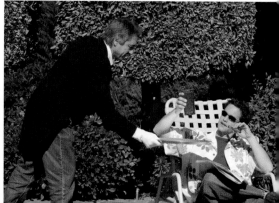

Santa Monica Promenade

Because of its proximity to the ministry office, we frequently go to Santa Monica's Third Street Promenade to film interviews. It's a favorite "fishing hole" for witnessing.

A homeless man takes the "Good Test."

Dale Jackson, our talented graphic artist.

This man believes we can influence the sun by our thoughts.

Ray interviews a lady and her friendly pet.

VIEWER'S QUESTION

"How were the interviewees selected?"

We wanted to get a cross section of humanity—from a businessman, to a punk, to a gang member, to an average everyday person. Some individuals tend to be intimidated by certain people, and seeing us witness to gang members or to a huge body builder can help others feel less fearful about approaching these types of people. We want to get across the wonderful fact that we are appealing to the conscience, rather than the intellect, which takes the "argument" out of the equation. All of humanity has the knowledge that it's wrong to lie, steal, etc., so they will nod in agreement with the Law. However, it does make interesting television to have colorful characters. It is fascinating to watch someone who has purple streaks in his hair, or who bursts into song on camera.

When it came to actually editing footage into particular programs, we did have a clear agenda. We wanted to equip the Christians who are watching, as well as present the entire gospel to any unsaved channel surfers. So the ideal is for an interview to be colorful, equipping, and convicting.

Todd Friel interviews for his radio program.

When Ray Comfort speaks,
people pretend to listen.

Todd Friel, 6'4", comes
down to Comfort level.

A Hollywood actress stops to talk about God.

This woman believes in reincarnation.

Duane's wife,
Yasmine, gives
her husband an
admiring glace.

Sharing with a congenial homosexual man
who was receptive to the things of God.

VIEWER LETTER

Learning from the lost

I recently saw "The Way of the Master,"
and it was riveting. I couldn't take my
eyes away when the couple was being
witnessed to by Ray and the guy kept
trying to defend himself. You could see
in his face he knew what Ray said was
true but he had too much pride to
admit he was wrong. It was very sad.

I am happy that a program leaves
the normal format and goes and talks to
real people—what a concept. We get a
great perspective from the unsaved. I
feel good about this program. There is
no desperation or ulterior motives, just
a positive, biblical point of view.

—Rachel

A young lady goes through the "Good Test."

Kirk demonstrates the Curved Illusion tracts.

MEETING RAY COMFORT — KIRK CAMERON

I REMEMBER THE first time I met Ray Comfort. I had recently listened to "Hell's Best Kept Secret" and read *Revival's Golden Key* [now titled *The Way of the Master*] and felt that I just had to meet the brilliant mind behind the message. We arranged to have lunch in Bellflower, CA. When I saw Ray, my first thought was, *There he is. Ray Comfort. The Theologian. The Genius.* Ray was friendly, even a bit goofy, and immediately led me (along with his daughter, Rachel, and associate Mark) into the lobby of the restaurant. I was stunned as Ray casually walked up to the hostesses, showed them a fake ID with his forehead stretched to over 12 inches high, and gathered a crowd of waiters by performing some sleight-of-hand magic tricks for them. *What a clown. I don't believe this,* I thought. I stepped back into the crowd of patrons, not wanting to be noticed (or associated with the clown). Then as the waitress walked us to our table, Ray took a detour and walked up to every table and in a friendly voice said, "Did you get one of these?" Then he did the unthinkable: he actually tossed gospel tracts on each table and walked away! I could hardly believe it. I was so embarrassed. I wanted to end the lunch right then and there—politely excuse myself, and leave. I was thinking, *Oh, no . . . he's one of those! I came here expecting to meet a brilliant theologian and instead I found a lunatic.*

After three hours of conversation with Ray, and seeing people actually enjoy reading the tracts (and then not only thanking Ray for them, but actually asking him for more!), my fears were quelled and I was firmly rooted in my appreciation for Ray, his family, and his ministry. . . but I still had lots of questions. We went back to his office and I asked a ministry worker why he handed out tracts. He looked down, thought for a moment, then replied, "Why not?" He told a story of how the day before, he had a wonderful conversation with a woman, after which he gave her a gospel tract called "Something to Think About." As he was walking out to his car, she ran after him, calling out, "Wait! I have to know why you gave this to me. Just the other night a family member had died, and I asked God to show me the right way. Is this an answer to my prayer?" For the first time, I understood how a well-written gospel tract could make a positive impression on a non-Christian and open the door for a meaningful witnessing encounter.

I knew then that I had much to learn from Ray Comfort and I resolved to never again refer to him as a lunatic (except when he puts that silly pen through his lip!).

Las Vegas

A colorful New Yorker in Las Vegas says that he doesn't have time for God.

This likeable man professed to be a Christian, but said that he hadn't read his Bible for two months. When challenged about gambling, he said that he would play Russian roulette for $10,000,000. When he grabbed hold of the gun (he didn't know it was a starter gun), Ray took it from his hand and challenged him about his priorities in life.

A Christian woman says she normally tells non-Christians that God has a wonderful plan for their lives.

WORDS OF COMFORT

WE WENT TO Las Vegas to shoot "The Greatest Gamble" episode. I told Kirk there was no way we would be able to film in an actual casino, because if a viewer noticed his local bank manager gambling in the background, it wouldn't be good for business. But God opened doors, and we opened the shoot with Kirk and me in the casino, sitting at a blackjack table. Kirk looked up at the camera, nudged me and said, "Um . . . it's not what it seems . . . we are actually here filming another episode of 'The Way of the Master.' We are going to ask people, 'What is the greatest gamble anyone can take?'"

We had a briefcase filled with Million Dollar Bill tracts, with a $20 bill on top of each bundle. We also had a starter gun (which looked like the real thing) on top of the money. We asked people if they would gamble their lives by playing Russian roulette (with three bullets in a six-shooter) for ten million dollars. One young one man was actually going to do it. He said, "Fifty-fifty chance for ten million dollars. Sure!" When he picked up the gun and pulled it toward his head, I grabbed his hand and said, "This is a fake gun. What are you doing? Do you love money more than your life?" It was an interesting interview.

Of course, the greatest gamble of all is to say that there is no Hell, because you are betting your eternal destiny on whether you are right.

These youths had been drinking alcohol for six hours before this interview.

Kirk witnesses to a group of Mormons.

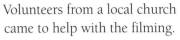

Reflecting on the day's shoot.

Duane, goofing around.

Volunteers from a local church came to help with the filming.

If you will not have death unto sin, you shall have sin unto death. There is no alternative. If you do not die to sin, you shall die for sin. If you do not slay sin, sin will slay you.

—CHARLES SPURGEON

Setting up at a scene in Las Vegas.

At a blackjack table, for the shoot on
"The Greatest Gamble."

POLICE DETOUR

SCOTTY AND HIS WIFE, Carol (our on-set photographer), had to finalize papers for a shooting permit with the Las Vegas police. They were apprehensive when they learned the police lieutenant wanted to talk to them about some "discrepancies."

As the secretary escorted them into the lieutenant's office, Scotty handed her a Million Dollar Bill tract. A few minutes later, while the lieutenant was questioning them about the permit, she reappeared in the doorway, interrupted the conversation, and motioned for Scotty to come outside. She then asked, "Could I please have another one of those million dollar bills?"

After the lieutenant's questions were answered, he asked what the show was about. Scotty, who was a little nervous about the eventuality of calling the lieutenant a "lying, thieving, adulterer-at-heart," began by telling the lieutenant that the premise of the show was to teach Christians how to share their faith . . . and then he took him through the Law. Here's the story in Scotty's own words:

"I meant to simply make the point and quickly move on because of the situation; but it ended up coming out differently. I wanted to use his first name, but as I began to speak, I couldn't remember it. All I could think of was his title. Because I had already started to speak, I had to finish or sound like a complete idiot, and with each word I spoke I realized it was coming out exactly the opposite of what I intended—which was making me pause between words, making it even worse! What ended up coming out was, 'So, . . . Lt. Williams, . . . by your own admission, . . . you are a lying, . . . thieving, . . . adulterer . . . at heart!'

"I couldn't have put him more on the spot if I tried. Not only that, but this was in front of my wife to boot. There was this long, awkward silence as I tried to think of how to recover. He simply nodded in agreement.

"Carol and I took him through the rest of the gospel, and he listened with interest. When we were through, he indicated that he had recently been thinking about these things and had determined to find out more. We were able to share quite a bit with him and answer a few questions. It was a significant conversation.

"As Carol and I walked out and talked about what had just happened, we realized that if nothing else, all the difficulties and hard work were worth it if the only point was for that man to hear the gospel and understand the depth of God's love for him. We gave him The Passion tract and the next day dropped off an *Evidence Bible*, as he didn't own a Bible.

"As it turned out, we ended up canceling the site we needed the permit for. We sometimes wonder why God allows us to go through difficulties and what seems to be extra work for nothing. But every once in a while, we get to see what's going on."

Alcatraz

Some of the gear for the shoot.

Food for the crew.

The prison guard dorms.

A group of native American Indians claimed Alcatraz for the Indian people. Their occupation began on November 20, 1969, and lasted until June 11, 1971.

VIEWER'S QUESTION

"How long on average does it take to set up a scene?"

Setup always takes time. For example, when we filmed at Alcatraz, the entire crew had to get onto the island to set up hours before we arrived. We would normally stay behind and go through the script together while the equipment was being set up, and would be called when they were ready for us. Even then, it was normal to have to wait another hour or two because a light wasn't quite right, or there were unforeseen last-minute sound problems. These were often caused by weather changes. Wind on the microphone or the sun coming from behind clouds were continual annoyances.

Alcatraz Island.

ALCATRAZ ISLAND — KIRK CAMERON

ON MAY 18, 2004, Ray and I met at the Los Angeles airport and got on the plane to meet our crew in San Francisco for the taping of three new episodes for the television program: "Alcatraz, Al Capone, and Alcohol"; "How to Witness to Someone Who Is Gay"; and "True and False Conversion."

Our first destination was the infamous prison isolated on "The Rock," where inmates such as "Baby Face" Nelson, Al "Scarface" Capone, and Robert "The Birdman" Stroud spend years behind bars. The Alcatraz episode is loaded with lots of cool history, information about famous escapes, and shots of the prison. The subject of the episode is breaking out of the unseen "prison" of sin that enslaves a sinner and holds him in its chains. Like Peter, asleep in Herod's prison and awaiting execution, most nonbelievers are "asleep" in their sins and unaware of their fate, and must be "awakened" by being "struck" by God's Law.

We rented Alcatraz for the entire evening and arrived at the island at 5:00 p.m., but we had to wait until it was deserted by the tourists before we could begin taping. We were deep in the prison at 11:00 p.m. when suddenly the power went out. It was pitch black and a bit uncomfortable until we found the light switch again. We finished just after midnight and took a water taxi back to San Francisco. Ray had the opportunity to witness to the security guard and the island ranger who oversaw our shoot. They were both very open to the gospel and the ranger even prayed with Ray to receive Jesus as Lord and Savior.

After a short night's sleep we had a delicious breakfast with some of our crew. A few of us also exercised our minds with some brain-squeezing theological questions, and then we were off to the Golden Gate Bridge for two more episodes. Well . . . almost.

We got a late start (about an hour) because our cameraman took us on the "scenic route" to the set by going over the Bay Bridge instead of the Golden Gate Bridge. (Ray and I are sure he didn't get lost—it was simply his great love for bridge architecture that compelled him to lead us in the opposite direction from our set. We love you, Ron. Thanks for the tour!)

The set for "How to Witness to Someone Who Is Gay" was located high above the Bay with a breathtaking view of the Golden Gate Bridge and the city. On top of the hill, the winds were high and presented some sound-quality issues, but our sound man (Scotty) made it work. Ray and I

Chatting with the ranger.

The view from the island.

A little makeup.

spent many hours writing this script, consulting several ex-homosexuals including one Christian man who "participated in this lifestyle for a lifetime." Their input was priceless and helped a great deal. We took tremendous care as we spoke about the very sensitive and prevalent issue of homosexuality. Many Christians have asked us how to share the gospel with someone who is "gay," and now we have a wonderful episode that addresses the subject in detail. It focuses on how to gently address the "root" of the problem instead of making the common mistake of offensively attacking the "branch" of a particular sin. It includes plenty of witnessing footage on the streets to demonstrate the teaching.

With only a couple of hours of sunlight remaining, we broke down the gear and set up for our next shoot on the beach below the bridge. The view was again phenomenal. We ate lunch on the fly and completed filming "True and False Conversion" just in time to return our rental car and make our flight home to Los Angeles.

I have worked on many television and film sets and I know that we at "The Way of the Master" have been so blessed. Our director, Duane, is so good and has such an incredibly artistic eye that every shot is cool and interesting to look at. Scotty (sound), Carol (photography), Ron (camera), and Louis (equipment), along with the rest of our crew and helpful volunteers, love the Lord and made this shoot a particularly memorable one for us.

Going over the script very late at night.

Getting ready to film the episode that speaks of sin being like a prison.

Shooting within the prison.

VIEWER LETTER

Witnessing to gays

I saw on TV a behind-the-scenes of "The Way of the Master" where a tour of your facility was given. At one point Kirk Cameron said a future program would be on how to witness to gays. That is interesting. I am gay. I have been with my lover for 16 years, I have 31 years background in the Assemblies of God, I have 988 weekly TV programs in Washington, 572 in the Portland area, and around 52 in Wisconsin. Just wonder how you figured out how to witness to gays. I have talked personally with about 700,000 homophobes and yet to find any that know what they are talking about when it comes to the Bible. Many are pastors and other ministers, college professors, Hebrew scholars with the highest degree of education on the Bible and ancient Hebrew, etc. So I am hoping you might be a rarity and can tell me about this "witnessing to gays."

—Unsigned

58

"HOMOSEXUALITY" SCRIPT

RAY: We would like to speak about an issue that is very prevalent in today's society, but one that must be dealt with in incredible sensitivity. It's the subject of homosexuality. In the past, many of us as Christians have been rightly accused of insensitivity, or even of having a "holier than thou" attitude when it comes to this issue.

KIRK: This is probably because we haven't shared the gospel with them biblically, and we have isolated homosexuality as being particularly wicked and failed to speak with love and compassion, as we should. They are often treated as though they are lepers. Remember, *all* sexual sin is offensive to God. Homosexual *and* heterosexual sin—adultery, homosexuality, fornication (sex before marriage), and even lust, something God considers to be adultery-of-the-heart—are sinful in His sight. So we should never have a condescending attitude toward any other human beings, regardless of their sexual preference.

I know people who are gay. I care about them very much, but in the past I have been terrified to witness to them because I didn't want to offend them. Perhaps you have the same concerns. So we are going to teach you a biblical way to reach out to someone who is gay.

RAY: The first question we should ask ourselves is, is homosexuality morally wrong? Let's look to the Scriptures and see what the Word of God says:

"Or do you not know that the unrighteous will not inherit the kingdom of God? Do not be deceived; neither fornicators, nor idolaters, nor adulterers, nor effeminate, nor homosexuals, nor thieves, nor the covetous, nor drunkards, nor revilers, nor swindlers, will inherit the kingdom of God." (1 Corinthians 6:9,10)

"For this reason God gave them over and abandoned them to vile affections and degrading passions. For their women exchanged their natural function for an unnatural and abnormal one, and the men also turned from natural relations with women and were set ablaze (burning out, consumed) with lust for one another—men committing shameful acts with men and suffering in their own bodies and personalities the inevitable consequences and penalty of their wrongdoing and going astray, which was [their] fitting retribution." (Romans 1:26,27)

But many gay people will ask, "Then why do I feel this way? Why would God allow me to have these feelings if they are wrong?" To answer that question, we must first understand that just because something *feels* right, doesn't mean it *is* right. Just because a man or woman *feels* like committing adultery, that doesn't mean it's right.

KIRK: Often gay people say that it's not a lifestyle they have chosen, but rather one they have by nature. They are right. They are that way. They were born that way "by nature"—the Bible says so. The truth is, we are *all* born with a sinful nature. It doesn't matter whether we have

The Bay Bridge.

San Francisco.

North of San Francisco.

homosexual tendencies, or heterosexual tendencies. We are all born with the *capacity* and desire to sin. We gravitate to sin as a moth gravitates toward a flame. That's why we must be born again with a new heart... with new desires...desires that are *pleasing* to God, which He will give to anyone who comes to Him in repentance and faith.

RAY: So, rather than take our moral guide by what *feels* good and seems natural to us, we must look to God's Word, because as the Bible says, the human heart is deceitful and can't be trusted—but *His* judgments are "righteous and true altogether."

V.O. [voice over] "There is a way which seems right to a man, but its end is the way of death." (Proverbs 14:12)

KIRK: The problem with the way many well-meaning Christians have tried to witness to their gay friends is that they've failed to see that homosexuality is simply one branch of sin on the deep-rooted tree of our sinful nature.

GRAPHIC OF TREE AND BRANCH (DALE)

Sometimes we as Christians look at the tree, see a branch that we perceive to be so offensive, and think that we should attack the branch—and the person naturally becomes defensive. I mean, think of how you'd feel if someone isolated one of your particular sins and grilled you on it. It would be like going up to a man who is 860 pounds and saying, "I'm a Christian. I want to talk to you about the sin of obesity." That would be insensitive, and we therefore shouldn't be surprised if we get a cold response. Instead, what we *should* do is do what Jesus did. He addressed the root cause of the problem, not just the branch of a particular sin. How did He do that? He used the Law, the Ten Commandments. Paul said that the Law was what showed him his sin in its true light and was the schoolmaster to lead him to Christ.

V.O. "But we know that the Law is good, if one uses it lawfully, realizing the fact that the law is not made for a righteous person, but for those who are lawless and rebellious, for the ungodly and sinners, for the unholy and profane, for those who kill their fathers or mothers, for murderers and immoral men and homosexuals and kidnappers and liars

and perjurers, and whatever else is contrary to sound teaching..." (1 Timothy 1:8–10)

RAY: Again, think of it like this. If the root of the sinful nature is dealt with, the branch of homosexuality (or whatever sin it may be) will wither and die, because its life source has been taken away. So if we care about someone, and want to see them *genuinely* converted, at the heart level, we must ignore the branch and go for the root.

INTERVIEWS—WITNESSING TO HOMOSEXUALS

Remember, our job is to plant the seed and someone else will water it, but it is God who changes the heart. I'm going to read a letter to you from a man who lived a gay lifestyle, but whose heart was changed by the power of God. Here is a letter from someone who "participated in this lifestyle for a lifetime":

> There is no such thing as a homosexual. There are people with homosexual desires...Our consciences continue to convict us, all the while we are ensnared by this life choice. And it IS a choice. The feelings & desires we responded to are complicated and seemingly come to us unbidden, but our acceptance of and following the dictates of these feelings is a choice. The rampant drug and alcohol use in the "gay" world are attempts to quiet the convictions of our consciences...God can take what is sinful and filthy, and turn it into something pure and holy, if we let him.

Conclusion: So there you have it. How do you witness to someone who is gay? The same way you would witness to someone who's not gay. Remember, we have all sinned and come short of the glory of God. Forget about the branch of homosexuality and go for the root of the sinful nature. This is the way of the Master. It's what Jesus did, and this is the way to reach this dying world for the Kingdom of God.

For more lessons on how to use the Ten Commandments to bring the knowledge of sin and lead a person to Christ, please get "The Way of the Master" Foundation Course or get *The Way of the Master* book at your local Christian bookstore. Or visit our website for free witnessing tools, books, CDs, and DVDs, at www.wayofthemaster.com.

San Francisco

Contemplative director.

Checking the shot on the hill overlooking the Golden Gate Bridge.

Praying before filming.

You are the light of the world. A city that is set on a hill cannot be hidden...Let your light so shine before men, that they may see your good works and glorify your Father in heaven.
—MATTHEW 5:14,16

Duane checks how things look through the viewing monitor.

Trying to hold the reflector board steady in strong winds.

High above the San Francisco Bay.

Despite the high winds, we get a "thumbs up" from Scotty for the sound.

Kirk shares a suggestion.

VIEWER'S QUESTION

"What is the most difficult thing about television production?"

Television production is so much more complex than producing radio programs. When doing audio recordings, if there is a blooper, it can be fixed in post-production. But it's not so easy with television. It has to be word, face, and body perfect. One of the greatest frustrations is when we would get something word perfect, but fail to end it with the right emphasis or expression—we would paint ourselves into a corner. Another frustration is when something was done perfectly—there were no mispronunciations, the expressions were correct, and the ending was just right—but then we would hear the director say, "Sound problems. Do it again."

Don't step back!

Someone flubbed his lines.

Another funny moment.

"The fish I caught was this big…"

Filming "True and False Conversion" at the base of the Golden Gate Bridge.

Ray makes a point.

Kirk makes a point about the point made by Ray.

THERE IS A WAY THAT SEEMS RIGHT

EXPERTS HAVE ALWAYS told us that if you are in an earthquake, the place of safety is to hide under a heavy table or some solid object. However, time has shown that in severe earthquakes, that action is what kills people. When a ceiling collapses, it falls onto the table, the table collapses and crushes whatever is underneath it. Consider these words from Doug Copp of the American Rescue Team International (ARTI), the world's most experienced rescue team:

> The first building I ever crawled inside of was a school in Mexico City during the 1985 earthquake. Every child was under their desk. Every child was crushed to the thickness of their bones. They could have survived by lying down next to their desks in the aisles. It was obscene, unnecessary, and I wondered why the children were not in the aisles. I didn't at the time know that the children were told to hide under something. Simply stated, when buildings collapse, the weight of the ceilings falling upon the objects or furniture inside crushes these objects, leaving a space or void next to them. This space is what I call the "triangle of life."

> The proven place of safety is therefore beside the table or solid object.

The world thinks that on the Day of Judgment they can shelter under the safety of good works. That seems right to them. It may make sense, but they are misguided. There is only one place of safety—in the Savior. They need the Law to show them that their philosophy is wrong. Dead wrong.

The Golden Gate Bridge.

"TRUE AND FALSE CONVERSION" SCRIPT

INTRO.

KIRK: Brice's friend. No Holy Spirit change. He said, "Christians themselves are proof that Christ cannot be the way."

RAY: If you don't believe there's no difference, look at these statistics. A poll taken some years ago revealed that 62% of Americans had a relationship with Jesus Christ that was "meaningful to them," but according to the book *The Day America Told the Truth*, 91% of us lie regularly at work or home. We found these quotes on an atheistic website under the heading "Christianity Does Not Work as Advertised." They were copied from the Barna Research Group:

- The divorce rate is no different for those who say they are born-again than for those who do not consider themselves religious.

- Most Christians' votes are influenced more by economic self-interest than by spiritual and moral values.

- Desiring to have a close, personal relationship with God ranked sixth among the 21 life goals tested among those who said that they were born-again, trailing such desires as "living a comfortable lifestyle."

"Are people's lives being transformed by Christianity?" Barna has asked. "We can't find evidence of a transformation."

KIRK: Too hard on Christians? Listen to what A. W. Tozer said: "It is my opinion that tens of thousands of people, if not millions, have been brought into some kind of religious experience by accepting Christ, and they have not been saved."

"The vast majority of people who are members of churches in America today are not Christians. I say that without the slightest fear of contradiction. I base it on empirical evidence of twenty-four years of examin-

ing thousands of people." —*Dr. D. James Kennedy*

RAY: Does the Bible address this issue? It does. Jesus: Tree by its fruit; good tree cannot bear evil, etc. He also said "many" on that Day, and in Mark 4:3–8, Jesus taught the crowd the well-known Parable of the Sower:

> Listen! Behold, a sower went out to sow. And it happened, as he sowed, that some seed fell by the wayside; and the birds of the air came and devoured it. Some fell on stony ground, where it did not have much earth; and immediately it sprang up because it had no depth of earth. But when the sun was up it was scorched, and because it had no root it withered away.
>
> And some seed fell among thorns; and the thorns grew up and choked it, and it yielded no crop. But other seed fell on good ground and yielded a crop that sprang up, increased and produced: some thirtyfold, some sixty, and some a hundred.

KIRK: When Jesus told His disciples the Parable of the Sower, they didn't understand what it meant. When they asked Him about it later, He said, "Do you not understand this parable? How then will you understand all the parables?" (Mark 4:13). In other words, the Parable of the Sower holds the key to unlocking the mysteries of all the other parables.

If there is one message that comes from the parable about the stony ground, the thorny ground, and the good ground, it is this: *When the gospel is preached, there will be true and false conversions.*

RAY: I used to think that the Parable of the Sower was simply telling us that when the gospel is preached, only one in four will respond—a 25% success rate. However, after searching the Scriptures, I don't think that anymore. I don't think Jesus gave us the parable as a consolation for disappointing evangelistic results. It contains keys to reaching the lost. Look at the true convert—the good soil hearer. Jesus said he hears and *understands*. There's the key. He comprehends the issues at stake. The others respond to the gospel, but without "understanding" appearing to come to Christ, but later falling away.

What is it then that will bring "understanding" to a sinner? It is the Law, which the Bible says is a "schoolmaster." The purpose of a "schoolmaster" is to bring knowledge. The Book of Romans tells us that the Law brings the "knowledge" of sin. It helps us clearly "understand" the issues that will "bring us to Christ."

Judas, it would seem, was a false convert. He was a hypocrite—a *pretender;* he had no idea who Jesus really was. When a woman—in an act of sacrificial worship—anointed Jesus with an expensive ointment, Judas complained that the ointment should have been sold and the money given to the poor. In his estimation, Jesus of Nazareth wasn't worth such extravagance; He was only worth about thirty pieces of silver. Moreover, the Bible tells us that Judas was lying when he said that he cared for the poor. He was actually a thief who so lacked a healthy fear of God that he was stealing money from the collection bag (John 12:6). Nevertheless, to all outward appearances, Judas was a follower and disciple of Christ.

KIRK: Once we realize that there will be true and false conversions when the gospel is preached, then the light of revelation begins to dawn on the rest of what Jesus taught in parables about the Kingdom of God. If one grasps the principle that true and false converts will be *alongside each other* in the Church, then the other parables also make sense: the Wheat and Tares (true and false converts), the Wise Virgins and the Foolish Virgins (true and false converts), and the Sheep and Goats (true and false converts).

Notice that the Good Fish and the Bad Fish were in the net *together.* Notice also that the *world* is not caught in the dragnet of the Kingdom of Heaven; they remain in the world. The "fish" that are caught are hearers who respond to the gospel—the evangelistic "catch." They remain together (the true and the false) until the Day of Judgment.

RAY: False converts *do* have a measure of spirituality; that is, they do resemble a true Christian. Judas certainly did—he was a classic false convert. He had apparently convinced the other disciples that he truly cared for the poor. And he *seemed* so trustworthy that they appointed him to be the treasurer—the one who looked after the finances. And when Jesus said, "One of you will betray Me," the disciples didn't point the finger at Judas; instead, they suspected themselves, saying, "Is it I, Lord?" That's why it's not surprising that so few of us would suspect that we are surrounded by false converts—those who fall into the "Judas" category.

KIRK: The tragedy is that most of those we commonly call "backsliders" are most likely not Christians at all. It's impossible to backslide when you've never slid forward in the first place. So we not only have many professing Christians who still serve sin, proving their false conversion, but to make matters worse, most of these also have a false sense of assurance. They think that they are heading for Heaven because they made a "decision," but their lives don't match up to what the Bible says a true follower of Christ should be like.

P. NASTY CLIP.

KIRK: How did Jesus do it? Mark 10:17, "Jesus having a bad day," etc.

RAY: Addressing the conscience. Romans 8. Carnal mind, enmity.

KIRK: Bill Bright 2%. We all have a moral responsibility. Please promote TWOTM book in your store.

Free DVD. www.wayofthemaster.com.

The false notion that they may be children of God while in a state of disobedience to his holy commandments, and disciples of Jesus though they revolt from his cross, and members of his true church, which is without spot or wrinkle, notwithstanding their lives are full of spots and wrinkles, is of all other deceptions upon themselves the most pernicious to their eternal condition for they are at peace in sin and under a security in their transgression.

—WILLIAM PENN

The famous Golden Gate Bridge.

VIEWER LETTER

Law for the proud

Not often do I find anything on TV to watch, but tonight after I put my kids to bed I turned on the TV to find something to relax to. What I found was not only interesting but enlightening and promising. Our country today scares me with the way we have turned from God. I feel we have to sleep in the beds we've made and truthfully it's not a pretty sight. I hope and pray this program will be blessed and go far for our "failing in faith" country. I have never looked at the biblical view the way it was put across in the program tonight: Law for the proud and grace for the humble. It's there, though, and so obvious I wonder why I never saw it before. May God bless your move to evangelize our nation!

—*Delores R.*

Checking the script to see which hand gesture to make next.

Spirit West San Diego

A young lady attending this Christian music festival looks despondent after being confronted with the biblical reality of true and false conversion. She had no assurance of salvation, no evident fruit of genuine salvation, no idea what happens to people after they die, and yet she clung to a prayer she prayed for forgiveness when she was four years old, saying, "But you can't lose your salvation!"

A lively interview.

Laura Spence (the wife of Mark Spence) tries her hand at an interview.

This young man (evidently "on fire") had all the right answers when it came to being a Christian.

This gentleman was adamant that someone was born again when he or she partook of the Mass. He maintained that the new birth, as described by Jesus in John 3, wasn't necessary for salvation. Those who were not born again would go to purgatory.

Eddie Kaulukukui steadies the camera. Eddie works with the ministry (while pursuing an acting career) and was able to join us for the day's shoot.

Even if I were utterly selfish and had no care for anything but my own happiness, I would choose, if God allowed, to be a soul winner, for never did I know perfect, overflowing, unutterable happiness of the purest and most ennobling order till I first heard of one who had sought and found a Savior through my means.

—CHARLES SPURGEON

Anna Jackson conducts an interview.

Mark Spence interviews.

VIEWER LETTER

"I can do this!"
I am 68 years old and, by God's grace, was saved 11 years ago. Recently my wife and I caught "The Way of the Master" program. Wow!!! In my years as a believer I attempted to witness to friends, family, and others with whom I came in contact. After turning off my family members (all unsaved), and all my "friends" would have nothing to do with me anymore, and offending the few strangers I tried to witness to, I gave up. After viewing the program I am greatly encouraged and have sent for several "Way of the Master" training materials. What a great approach! I can do this! I will feel comfortable in witnessing and my wife and I are now considering starting a discipleship program in our church. Thank you so much for this program!!!

—Frank L., Indiana

West Hollywood

West Hollywood has a large gay community.

Men with men, women with women (Romans 1:26,27).

Against nature.

Ray witnesses to a bisexual man.

 Kevin was gay and also an atheist.

Kirk asks if he thinks homosexuality is a "moral" issue.

The only way we can know whether we are sinning is by knowing His Moral Law.
—Jonathan Edwards

BURLY "GIRLY MEN"
— KIRK CAMERON

TO FILM THE episode called "How to Witness to Someone Who Is Gay," we traveled to the epicenters of America's homosexual community: San Francisco and West Hollywood, California. We met in a grocery store parking lot in "Boys Town, USA" to prepare for our interviews. As we watched gay men stroll past us holding hands, enter gay bars and nightclubs, greet each other with cutesy kisses, and snuggle up to one another on the streets, all of us guys on the production team had the same thoughts. We knew our manhood was in jeopardy (in that neighborhood, we too might be viewed as being gay!). Almost simultaneously, we all began acting ultra-manly. Our voices got deeper, our stride was unmistakably straight, and we made sure our wedding rings were showing. We wanted to make it clear that we were not "girly men." No. Rather, we were strong, muscular, and very *manly* men. Ray even began practicing a crushing handshake combined with a *very* masculine sounding, **"Hello. My name is Ray."**

This man became upset during the interview, then returned about ten minutes later and tried to disrupt another interview. Anna had to hold him at bay.

I suppose we did this also to reassure ourselves that if we happened to get into a heated argument with a gay man who wanted to fight, we could easily defend ourselves against our softer, more sensitive adversaries. Boy, were we wrong.

Walking down the street we noticed, coming toward us, some tall, very muscular, burly looking guys, some dressed in tight blue jeans and cowboy boots, and looking quite intimidating. These guys were no little "girly men." They were huge, hulking, hairy homosexuals! Our imaginations ran wild. Fear gripped our hearts. We were sure these guys knew where we were and all they wanted to do was wrap their giant hands around our little necks. I wanted to go home. Ray put on sunglasses to remain "anonymous." Our director, Duane, laughed at our ridiculous behavior and started recruiting interviewees.

Kirk wondering what upset the man being interviewed.

Our interviews turned out great. These big guys were (for the most part) very nice, respectful, and kind. Only one fellow got upset and looked like he might start throwing punches. But he was just a slight little guy (whose wrists didn't look strong enough to hold a cup of coffee, let alone support a fist), so we weren't worried. After all, we were MANLY MEN!

This sign was draped over the front of the local gay church.

This man's marriage fell apart so he decided to "try men." He said it worked, and now he's happy. He was very surprised that the man being interviewed before him became rather angry. However, he also became very agitated when he was taken through the Law.

Nonetheless, this man still wanted to have his picture taken with Kirk and Duane.

WORDS OF COMFORT

I WAS SITTING in the Los Angeles airport waiting to fly to Nashville, and offered a tract to a large man who was sitting two seats away from me. He coldly said, "Keep it." I put it back in my pocket and then offered him another tract. Most people take this one if they refuse the first. It looks like a business card, but it says, "Department of Annoyance, Director." It makes the first offer make sense. I deepen my voice and say, "This is where I'm from" and hand it to them. The air of authority makes them take it, and almost everyone laughs when they see the "annoyance" part. Not this man. He just repeated, "Keep it." A moment later he got up and left and a younger man took his seat.

I have learned that if someone throws you off, you have to find another horse and get right back into the saddle. So I ignored my sense of rejection and the fear of it happening a second time, and I slid a Million Dollar Bill tract across the seat, saying, "Here's a million dollars for you—it's great when you get the change." This man burst out laughing. That made me feel good, so I asked, "Where are you from?" He was from Texas and was going back home for his father's surprise fiftieth birthday party. He had been in Los Angeles for five

months pursuing an acting career, working as a waiter in a Hollywood hotel.

I told him that I co-hosted a TV program with the actor Kirk Cameron. When he said that he had actually seen the program, I asked if he'd had a Christian background. "Catholic." I asked, "Have you been 'born again'—do you know what that means?" He answered, "That's when you believe that Jesus died on the cross for you and you ask Him into your heart. I believe all that." I explained that the difference between believing that Jesus died for you and trusting in Him was like the difference between believing in a parachute and putting it on. I said, "You know what helped me? It was this little test: *Would you consider yourself to be a good person?*" He said that he did, so I took him through the Ten Commandments. He had lied, but when I asked him what that made him he said a predictable, "Human." We live in an age of unaccountability. It's the "It's not my fault" age. Adrian was only "human." He had weaknesses like every other human being and was therefore not really accountable. But the truth is, every man will give an account of himself to God, and this is why each Christian needs to be like Nathan the prophet and say, "You are the man!" and one way to do that is to have the person acknowledge what he is. I said to Adrian, "What would you call me if I told blatant lies?" He said, "A liar." We both smiled when I said that it sure is easier to see other people's sins. He had also stolen, blasphemed, and looked with lust. Yet he still thought that he would go to Heaven, so I explained the justice of God to him, then the cross.

He soberly said, "That made me think." I then explained that I had addressed his conscience rather than his intellect. I said, "It does make us think, because the conscience agrees with each of the Commandments. If I told you that I had a cure to lymph node cancer, and gave it to you, you would probably say, "What are you doing? What do I want this for?" But if I instead took the time to convince you that you had the disease, when I offered you the cure, you would appreciate it."

We then prayed together. I gave him my email address, a "Hell's Best Kept Secret" CD, a copy of "The Way of the Master" private screening, a copy of *The Evidence Bible*, and a book I had written called *101 Things Husbands Do to Annoy Their Wives* to give to his dad for his birthday. He was so grateful that I had spoken to him, and I was so thankful that I didn't listen to my fears.

On the flight to Nashville, I sat next to a 78-year-old man named Earl and his wife, Helen. I felt a twinge of fear because I respect older men and feel a little uncomfortable telling them what they should and shouldn't be doing. I said that I was an author and handed Helen a complimentary copy of *101 Things Husbands Do to Annoy Their Wives*. Earl and I then chatted about his background. I told him that I was going to speak at a Christian conference, and asked if he had a Christian background. He said he was an "unbeliever," and laughed.

I asked if he ever thought about his mortality—the fact that he was going to die. "Not much." I said, "You know what helped me? It was the Ten Commandments," and shared with him about lust being adultery, etc. I said that if God saw my thought-life and He was going to judge me by that standard, I would end up in Hell, not Heaven. His reaction was to smile and say, "You know how I deal with all of that? I don't believe it."

A few minutes earlier the flight attendant had asked what I wanted to drink, so I said that I would like hot chocolate with cream and nuts scattered across the top. She smiled and said, "Actually, we do have hot chocolate," and she even brought me an extra container of hot water. I wasn't too excited about the extra water because I suffer from "spill-drinkinson's disease."

As I moved the trash on my tray table away from me, the water container fell toward us and spilled hot water on both Earl and me. So I said, "Well, now we are *both* in hot water. Never mind, though. Let's not believe it happened."

Meanwhile, I could hear Helen laughing as she read the book. He asked me if my wife or I had written it. When I said that I was

Kirk reasons with this young lady, who was brought up in a Christian church and thinks that she might be gay.

This young man had left San Francisco to live in the gay district of West Hollywood.

Kirk witnesses to a gay man as two others listen in.

These three were in a band, and the leader (on the left) referred to the couple holding hands as his "b-tches."

the author, he mumbled something about me being a traitor.

From then on he was extra friendly and kept asking me questions about the things of God. I took him more thoroughly through the Commandments, then the cross, and thanked him for being so gracious and listening. He said, "You're welcome. Not many people have talked to me about this." He was grateful that I had spoken to him, and I was so thankful that I didn't listen to my fears.

When Kirk and I produced the program on how to witness to homosexuals, we came up short on interviews, so we decided to visit the homosexual district of West Hollywood. The day we were due to go there, I was a little nervous. As I was driving there with the camera crew, someone asked if I was nervous. I said, "I share my courage with others and keep my fear to myself." That was a great truth I learned from Robert Louis Stephenson. Just after that, Kirk called and said, "I'm nervous." I said, "So am I."

When we arrived, it wasn't what I expected. The gay district had a festive atmosphere, with men walking hand in hand and greeting one another with long hugs, and women passionately kissing each other. The area was upper class, clean, and tidy. It was a "sanitized Sodom."

I saw two men sitting together, so I walked up to them and said, "Hi. We're doing a TV program on America's spirituality and we want to get the perspective from the gay community. Are you two gay?"

Their names were Kevin and Ryan. Kevin was homosexual and Ryan was bisexual. Ryan didn't want to be on TV, so I called the crew over and Kirk interviewed Kevin.

I went over to sit next to Ryan and asked if he had a Christian background. His mother was Christian and his father was Catholic. He said that he had been pleading with God in prayer to take away his homosexual tendencies. I said, "You know what helped me? It was the Ten Commandments," and I took him through the Law, and into the cross. I told him that he needed a new nature, prayed with him, and then left him with some literature to help him. He was so grateful, and I was so thankful that I didn't listen to my fears.

Have you ever noticed that when you turn on a light, darkness leaves? The two are incompatible. It's the same with fear and love. Love casts out fear. When we turn on the light of God's love, fear can't stay. It has to leave. The key is to let love cause you to think of the terrifying fate of the person to whom you want to witness.

Paralyzing and tormenting fear isn't from God, but it can work for your evangelistic good. It can make you trust in God. Fear shows us that we are weak, and it causes us to call on God for His help. So don't let your fears discourage you. Instead, let them drive you to Him who gives courage, and in so doing, your greatest weakness then becomes your greatest strength.

Some individuals we saw were more colorful than others. This man's partner said that a personality took him over every now and then, and he felt compelled to dress as a woman and walk the streets. He wouldn't stand still long enough to let us talk with him.

VIEWER'S QUESTION

"Why do you give grace to the proud?"

Biblical evangelism is always Law to the proud and grace to the humble. A. W. Pink said, "Just as the world was not ready for the New Testament before it received the Old, just as the Jews were not prepared for the ministry of Christ until John the Baptist had gone before Him with his claimant call to repentance, so the unsaved are in no condition today for the Gospel till the Law be applied to their hearts, for 'by the Law is the knowledge of sin.' It is a waste of time to sow seed on ground which has never been ploughed or spaded! To present the vicarious sacrifice of Christ to those whose dominant passion is to take fill of sin, is to give that which is holy to the dogs." We sometimes gave grace to proud people on the program for two reasons. First, many Christians who tune into the program don't understand the importance of using the Law to reach the lost. We want to convince them that it is both biblical and very necessary. We are aware they would be horrified if we didn't tell sinners "the good news," especially after laying the Law on them. Our aim is for them to use the Law also, and we don't want them to write us off for what they perceive as a harsh, legalistic, or unbiblical approach. The second reason is more important. Non-Christians also tune into "The Way of the Master," and we want them to hear the gospel and be saved. So it was a slight dilemma for us, and we hope that our regular viewers will understand why we do this.

VIEWER LETTER

Dear Kirk and Ray,

I can't even begin to thank you enough for your ministry. I am sixteen years old, and I love all of your tracts, books, and videos. I had been reading *Revival's Golden Key* [now titled *The Way of the Master*], and I was sitting in front of the computer reading one of your columns. My eyes filled with tears as I realized that I wasn't truly saved! I had grown up in a Christian home, I witnessed every week, I did every Christian thing possible, but I had never been brought to salvation through the law. I guess I never really wanted to examine myself and face the facts. The funny thing is, it was on April 1, 2004, that I truly prayed for forgiveness—April Fool's Day. I had only been fooling myself! Thank you, thank you, thank you! I am now trying to live my life to please God, out of gratitude! God has softened my heart, and has truly given me a compassion for those who are lost. I get so excited every time I watch you witness. I want to do that! I can't wait to get out in this world and hand out tracts. Thank you from the very bottom of my heart!
—*Jacqueline*

Rainbow Club

Two men talk about their thoughts on the afterlife.

This man lived for alcohol, but argued that he wasn't an alcoholic. This interview was used in "Alcatraz, Al Capone, Alcohol."

AT THE RAINBOW Bar shoot there were several funny incidents, although that was probably the most spiritually "dark" place I'd been in years. At one point Ray was just beginning an interview when he learned the man was from Texas. It's always interesting to hear different people's accents, so Ray

DROWNING IN THIN AIR

asked the man, "What would you say if you were drowning and you wanted the lifeguard to save you?" Ray wanted to get the man to say the word "Help," because he was trying to see if the man's strong accent would divide the word into two syllables, "Hey-yulp." But instead of simply saying, "Help," this man, who seemed a bit eccentric to begin with, started to act out as if he were drowning. He was flailing his hands around in the air as if he were trying to stay above water, while producing gurgling sounds and screams. It was such an unexpected reaction to such a simple question that I couldn't help laughing—really loudly! Just picture it: it's the middle of the night, on an L.A. street corner, and a camera crew is filming a man who's acting like he's drowning in thin air!

—*Anna Jackson*

WORDS OF COMFORT

WE DECIDED THAT we needed some interviews regarding the subject of alcohol, so we inquired about filming at a famous Hollywood restaurant. This was reputed to be a place frequented by a number of well-known stars. The owners wanted $1,000 to film for the evening, but we thought it would be worth it, so we decided to do it.

What a dark place it was! Even though we were able to get some interesting interviews, we felt spiritually heavy as we drove home in the early hours of the morning. It really was a "den of iniquity." The patrons were weird, proud, obnoxious, foul-mouthed, and condescending. They were drunken, drugged, and dressed sensually. The music was loud and horrible, the rooms were dark, and the atmosphere was oppressive.

I was pleased that we were even getting to drive home. A week earlier we conducted interviews in West Hollywood in the homosexual community that caused some verbal abuse by one angry man. One of our team had to physically hold him back while I continued interviewing other people. Another gentleman walked away from me during an interview, and then came back a little later and did lewd acts. So on this night, I had the thought that I may not make it back from a dark place where I was stirring up demons by witnessing to the folks where they made their residence. In such close quarters it would be very easy to slip a knife into a back.

As we drove home, I had the thought that I never wanted to go back to that place again. We all felt like having a good wash. I decided to call our photographer to encourage her. She's just a little thing, about five feet tall and very quiet. She didn't say much all evening. She just followed us around, snapping pictures. No doubt she was feeling as oppressed as we were, so I called and said, "Carol, thank you so much for coming to such a horrible place tonight. I apologize for all the filthy language." She sounded upbeat and said, "I was interested and fascinated. They are the type of people Jesus came to seek and save." How true that is. It's easy to forget.

HAND OVER MOUTH

ANOTHER INCIDENT during the Rainbow Bar shoot involved this really arrogant evolutionist. He was a long-haired guy wearing a leather jacket, who claimed to be a doctor and could speak in techno-babble a mile long . . . but most of what he was saying was purely nonsensical. In the middle of Ray's interview with this man, I had become so involved in listening to the conversation that I just blurted out, "But that is a *corruption* of the existing DNA information. There has *never* been a documented case of *any* new information being added . . ." Ray turned around to me half-laughing and said, "Anna!" Then I realized that my thoughts had popped right out of my mouth and spoiled the interview they were *filming!* I think I kept my hand over my mouth for the rest of that one.

—*Anna Jackson*

A university professor argues the case for evolution.

Save some, O Christians! By all means, save some. From yonder flames and outer darkness, and the weeping, wailing, and gnashing of teeth, seek to save some! Let this, as in the case of the apostle, be your great, ruling object in life, that by all means you might save some.

—CHARLES SPURGEON

Boxing Ring

EZ, sitting in for camera angles before the shoot.

The opening shot of the show.

WORDS OF COMFORT

AFTER SOME DISCUSSION, we came to the conclusion that Christians who see "The Way of the Master" may get the impression that every time we share the gospel, people are kind and responsive, and many immediately receive Christ. It would be nice if that were the case, but in real life it doesn't happen that way. So we decided to show some of the "failures" we have recorded on film—cuts where people walked off during interviews, where they became angry, and where some even spat at us or hit us. This episode, called "When Things Go Wrong," is intended to serve as an encouragement, so if you are persecuted or rejected for sharing Christ, you can see that it is biblically normal and you shouldn't be discouraged. Duane had the idea to film at a boxing ring, to remind each of us that we are in a very real *fight* for the souls of men and women.

Flexing a little muscle.

Duane, trying his hand.

Joey is a professional boxer who was training when we filmed in the ring. It turned out that he was a Christian who became a boxer while in his forties, to support his family.

THIRD TIME'S A CHARM

KIRK AND RAY wanted me to do a short fill-in for the episode "When Things Go Wrong." They were going to film me explaining something that had gone wrong in an earlier episode.

Take one: Since I was the sound man, they wanted me to hold my equipment. I often wear my headphones around my neck when not in use, so that's how they wanted me to do the shot. After several takes I finally got it right and was glad it was over . . . or so I thought. When they checked the footage, there was something wrong— with the sound, of all things! It was muffled and unusable. I discovered that wearing the headphones around my neck like that covered the lapel mic under my shirt and muffled the sound! That's what happens when the sound man isn't doing the sound. Oh, well—it is an episode about "when things go wrong," and they certainly seemed to be going that way.

Take two: We made another attempt in front of some really cool-looking, rusty old cars. This time I wore the headphones further back on my neck so they wouldn't muffle the sound. The sound was fine; but with me leaning back in the chair and the camera at a low angle, I looked like Buddha doing an impression of Frankenstein with a couple of big black bolts coming out of my neck. The content really wasn't what was wanted anyway, so we had to do it again!

Take three: We set up in the production room. This time I was *standing up,* I was *holding* the headphones in my hand, the sound had been checked, the camera was at the correct angle, and the content was right. Everything was good to go. I was in the middle of my third or fourth take and could tell that this was the one! Suddenly, the lights changed. Brandon Martin, one of our telephone operators, was holding a light for us, and he moved the light. It was too close to the producer's shirt and the shirt started to smoke from the heat. Before the whole thing went up in flames, Brandon moved the light, and needless to say I had to do it again!

After all the things that went wrong while filming "When Things Go Wrong," we finally did complete the 60-second fill-in for the episode at who knows what cost, and at great jeopardy to the producer's shirt, in record time! Sorry, Duane. Hope it was worth it.

—Stuart ("Scotty") Scott

Filming the clip "Don't throw in the towel."

Kirk—against the ropes.

CUE CARDS: A BLESSING AND A CURSE — KIRK CAMERON

DURING EACH TAPING, we often use cue cards to help us remember our lines. These are large cards held by the side of the camera with handwritten notes, rotated one after another to remind us of what to say. While these cards can be very helpful for those moments when you forget what to say next, they can also be the cause of the director calling out, "Cut! Let's try it again." This is because when you forget your lines and think, *Oh, no! What comes next?* and then shift your eyes from the camera to the cards to begin reading, you get that "deer in the headlights" look on your face. It always happens no matter how hard you try not to let it. Then, once you look to the cards, you cannot look back into the camera because the change of focus will reveal to the audience that you were actually reading instead of just "speaking." So I've found that the solution is to thoroughly memorize your talk the night before and use as few cue cards as possible. And when you refer to them during a take, you must discipline yourself to merely *glance past* the words (as though a bird flying by caught your attention) and then continue speaking directly into the camera.

So if you ever see Ray or I with that laser beam stare off to the side of the camera and a blank expression on our faces while we are speaking, you'll know why.

VIEWER LETTER

"The happiest man on earth"
I am compelled to write to you with my deepest thanks for your ministry. Two years ago my wife brought home your book and a tape ("Hell's Best Kept Secret"). I read your book and listened to the tape twelve times. I could not believe it. I cried and was angry at myself all at the same time. I could not believe what you came up with, and I was mad that I had read Romans so many times and did not see it. I preach at prisons and drug centers here and I took your advice, with unreal results. Last week nine murderers and rapists ran to the front and fell on their knees. Most were weeping like babies, some begging for mercy. Tuesday fifteen women burst into tears and some literally fell to the ground...I am the happiest man on earth, because of you. I am leading 10 to 50 souls to Christ every week now and I am looking to sweep this state in the next two years.

—*M. W. Smith*

Going over the script.

Rocky VI.

VIEWER'S QUESTION

"Whose chairs are those, and why do you use them?"

The chairs that we used in the first few episodes belonged to Kirk and his wife, Chelsea. He would bring them to each shoot in his car. One day we noticed that they were starting to get a little damaged, so we purchased two new chairs that were similar to the originals. The chairs haven't been used in every shoot. That was our original intention, but we decided to change the look of the episodes a little for season two.

AS THE GENERAL Manager of "The Way of the Master," it has always been my great delight to be involved with the production of our television program. With the completion of each new episode I am struck with the realization that God is allowing us to be a part of something that is impacting both Christians and non-Christians in life-changing ways. It is especially encouraging when we receive letters written by viewers from different parts of the world telling us how God has used "The Way of the Master" to stir their hearts to seek and save the lost. There is no greater honor than being used by God to make a global impact for His glory. I find great pleasure in being able to watch a particular episode develop through the various stages of the production process. It is amazing to see mere concepts transform into eye-opening, tangible realities that will be preserved and passed down for generations to come. It is an indescribable thrill to be about our Father's business.

—Emeal ("EZ") Zwayne

A light moment, after the shoot.

Ozzfest

WE NEEDED TO get some applicable interviews for "The Satanic Influence" episode, so we applied for the necessary permits and visited an Ozzie Osborne "Ozzfest" in San Bernardino, California. These interviews were very colorful, and some were very demonic. They made ideal footage for the show.

This girl came under such conviction, she walked away from the interview.

Filming a "filler" before the interviews begin.

An EZ interview.

MASS HYPNOSIS

OZZFEST WAS an interesting time. We went there primarily to get interviews for the second-season show on Satanism. So when we began the interviews, I think we were all expecting a lot of people to be saying, "Yes, I worship Satan." At least that's what *I* was expecting. But what we found instead were people who were walking around with images of Satan on their shirts, Satan tattooed on their skin, making the sign of Satan with their hands, and singing "Hail Satan,"... but who were so deceived that they'd tell us, "Satan doesn't really exist." It was like watching some sort of peculiar mass hypnosis—sort of like going to a strawberry growers convention where a group of attendees are busily filling up on strawberries, but saying between bites, "There is no such thing as a strawberry."
—*Anna Jackson*

Pastor Joe Schimmel, producer of the well-known video "They Sold Their Souls for Rock and Roll," came with us on the shoot, and kindly gave us powerful footage to use in our episode.

VIEWER'S QUESTION

"Did you have any interesting reactions from passersby while you were interviewing?"

The most interesting reactions of passersby were at the Ozzfest rock concert in Southern California. Almost every interview had people in the background yelling obscenities. These weren't directed at us, they were simply shouted out because of the presence of the cameras.

One man we interviewed became a little upset by something that was said to him. At that moment a drunken passerby decided he would join in the interview uninvited. The man we were speaking to exploded in anger and lashed out at him with his fist. Then he turned back to us to continue the discourse. We thought we would be next. We used that footage in the episode "When Things Go Wrong."

Ron Meade tries his hand at being in front of the camera, for a change.

This man said "$%@!* Christianity!" and walked away from the interview.

Ron interviews a colorful character.

EZ interviews.

A porn producer talks about how he believes his industry benefits humanity.

A hardened and bitter "backslider" (false convert).

This Roman Catholic man became intensely concerned about his eternal salvation.

HOW WE GET INTERVIEWS

YOU MIGHT WONDER how we go about setting up the "on-the-street" interviews that are a big part of each program. When I go on location with the crew, this is usually the job I get to do.

When I'm trying to get interviews, I look for people who seem to be taking their time and who appear outgoing. I may also be given other instructions, such as, "We're trying to interview college kids," or "We want to talk to married people with kids."

Once I find someone who might be a fit, I walk up and greet them, then explain that we're doing interviews for a worldwide television show, and we'd like to get them on TV. Most people say no. So I say, "Well, then, here's your consolation prize," and I hand them a tract—usually a Million Dollar Bill. Then I go on to the next person.

When someone says, "Okay," they usually want to know what the interview is about. I really don't want to say, "We're going to use the Ten Commandments to circumnavigate your intellect and speak directly to your conscience, hopefully convicting you of sin so that you'll see your need to repent and trust in Jesus Christ and be saved from eternal Hell." If I do I'm not going to get many interviews ... so I usually tell them, "We're asking questions about spirituality, life after death, that sort of thing." If they ask, "What are the questions?" I say that I can't tell them, because we want to get their spontaneous reaction on camera.

The next question they usually ask is, "What TV show is this for? What channel is it on?" I try to avoid telling them the name of the show by saying, "We're on multiple channels and satellite networks. You can check us out online at WOTMworldwide.com for schedules and listings." I don't want to say the name of the show because then they immediately ask, "Is that a Christian show?" If people are anti-Christian, we're probably going to lose the chance to go through the gospel with them.

If they agree to do the interview, I have them sign a "name and likeness release form," then I walk them over near the camera crew, staying far enough away that they can't hear the interview that's going on. I'll usually engage them in small talk until it's time for their interview. Then I introduce them to whoever is doing the interview, and head out to find the next interview subject.

The job of "interview wrangler" requires an outgoing personality and a thick skin, because you're going to get a lot of rejections. But it's so much fun, I go every time I get a chance!

—*Anna Jackson*

A volunteer "signs off" prospective interviewees.

Santa Monica Promenade

A bird with a man under its feet.

Ray interviews a native of Sweden.

Kirk illustrates the Curved Illusion tracts.

This man seemed subdued during his interview.

This young woman was very firm in her spiritual beliefs and wasn't open to the gospel.

This man, a hermaphrodite who insisted that his name was "Fiona," burst into tears as he was challenged by God's Law, and walked off in anger. Ray ran after him and gave him $10 (he said he was hungry), but the man threw the money down. Ray picked it up, chased after him, and stuffed it into his hand. The man took it, but ten minutes later walked past Ray and deliberately snubbed him.

Ask Paul why [the Law] was given. Here is his answer, 'That every mouth may be stopped, and all the world may become guilty before God' (Romans 3:19). The Law stops every man's mouth. I can always tell a man who is near the kingdom of God; his mouth is stopped. This, then, is why God gives us the Law—to show us ourselves in our true colors.
—D. L. MOODY

Initially shocked to realize that she had sinned, this woman's mouth was stopped as she recognized her guilt.

This man said he had been thinking about these things before Ray talked with him, and their meeting was "fate." He committed his life to Christ.

When he speaks a lie, he speaks from his own resources, for he is a liar and the father of it. (John 8:44)

Unsaved people live in the kingdom of darkness. It's as simple as this: if we are serving sin, we are serving Satan. Our appetites are unclean. We desire pig food. Consider what we crave. Think of the contents of the average soap opera or prime-time television show—adultery, jealously, lust, fornication, rape, gossip, and greed. Or the average movie today with its violence, filthy language, explicit sex, and graphic murder.

Kirk decides to roast his shoe.

Look at the covers of magazines in bookstores and supermarkets. They are "soft-core" pornography, which a few years ago was considered hard-core and hidden from young eyes. Think of video games that kids crave—they are extremely violent and sexually perverted. Think of most rock music, with its explicit sexuality, its blasphemy, and its dark satanic side. Consider the Internet's multi-billion-dollar hard-core porn industry, or how the average person uses filthy words and blasphemy in everyday speech. Life in the dirty pigsty is normal, natural, and completely acceptable.

Yes, Satan is the god of this world, and he has deceived millions. But his deception hasn't stopped there. It has moved into the Church. Despite the fact that the Bible tells us Satan is real, he's a deceiver, and he is the god of this world who blinds minds, look at what has happened in the Church: according to the Barna Research Group, in 2004 an incredible 50 percent of those who profess to be "born again" actually deny Satan's existence.

That's unbelievable! Despite the revelation of Scripture, 50 percent of those who profess to be born again don't believe Satan is even real. And the scary thing about it is that if you deny that he exists, you let your guard down—you let him bring in deception. And the easiest

place to corrupt the Church is at the point of entry...to poison the evangelistic message that brings people into the Kingdom of God.

That's what has happened. We haven't been vigilant. We have allowed Satan to contaminate the biblical method of evangelism. We have allowed certain "ministers of righteousness" within the Church to move away from Scripture. They refuse to use the Law (the Ten Commandments) to bring the knowledge of sin (as Jesus did) and to show sin to "be exceedingly sinful." This is despite the fact that even the apostle Paul said he didn't know what sin was without the Law. They say that they have found a shortcut to bring people to salvation. They leave out the Law and instead take the prodigal son back to the father, without showing him that his appetites are unclean.

Remember that in the story Jesus told, the son "came to his senses" when he realized that he desired pig food. That's what made him want to go back to his father and say, "I have sinned against heaven and in your sight. Make me your hired servant." In the name of sensitivity, modern preachers don't let that happen. So instead of the professed convert saying to the Father, "I have sinned against Heaven. Make me Your servant," he goes to God and says, "I have run out of money. Give me some more. You be my servant."

The crew gathers for a close-up by the fire, on a cool night.

And that's

what's wrong with the modern Church. It is filled with unconverted people who have never seen that their sinful appetites are unclean. Modern preachers have left out the Law, and so we have multitudes in pulpits and in pews who don't see sin as exceedingly sinful. They look on God as their servant. Instead of saying, "Make me Your servant," they say, "Give me more!"

Aleister Crowley (who died in 1947) is considered to be the father of modern Satanism. In his publication called *The Book of the Law*, he sums up the essence of Satanism. It is: "do what thou wilt shall be the whole of the Law."

And that sums up the desires of many who profess to have faith in Jesus Christ. Their lack of concern for the lost shows that something is radically wrong. They have never given up their selfish will and cried, "Not my will, but Yours be done." They have never sought to serve God by doing His will in reaching out to the unsaved.

Remember that Bill Bright said only 2 percent of the contemporary Church in America share their faith regularly with others. All they want is what they can get from God—health, wealth, and prosperity. Listen to most modern preaching. It caters to nothing but selfishness. It's self-seeking, self-serving, and self-centered. The modern Church has become the last days' Laodicean church, which says that it's rich and in need of nothing, but in truth it is poor, blind, wretched, miserable, and naked.

How can this great multitude be awakened to this deception? Simply by helping them look into the mirror of the Ten Commandments—by seeing themselves under the light of God's Law. Every professing Christian should obey the admonition to "examine yourself to see if you are in the faith." But many won't. They think they are saved because they call Jesus "Lord" and do works in His name. They will wait until the Day of Judgment and cry, "Lord, Lord, we did many wonderful works in Your name," and Jesus will say to them, "I never

WORDS OF COMFORT

I HAD THE interesting experience of interviewing a representative from the "Church of Satan." One of their tenets is to be friendly to anyone they meet…but if that person offends them, they are to "destroy" them. It gave me great consolation to know that I had a wonderful camera crew with me—guys who were not only buff, but also faithful men of God. I was confident that if a knife was pulled and I was attacked during the interview…they would make sure that it was filmed from every angle.

After we filmed I gave the man a box of chocolates and a financial gift for his time. The money was slipped into one of

our butterfly tracts. A professing atheist, he emailed later saying, "Please tell [Ray] his butterfly gave us quite a surprise as [we merged] onto the freeway. I almost got to commune with God, but probably not in the way that was intended. But afterwards we had a good laugh and we always appreciate a little mirth."

There was a little tension at first, but the interview went well. Please pray for his salvation (his name is Jack). One of the stipulations of the interview was that I wasn't allowed to try to make him "see the light." We combined that clip with interviews from the Ozzie Osborne rock festival.

knew you; depart from Me, you who practice lawlessness!" They are still in their sins.

Martin Luther said, "The first duty of the gospel preacher is to declare God's Law and show the nature of sin." Then he said, "This now is the Christian teaching and preaching, which God be praised, we know and possess, and it is not necessary at present to develop it further, but only to offer the admonition that it be maintained in Christendom with all diligence. For Satan has attacked it hard and strong from the beginning until present, and gladly would he completely extinguish it and tread it under foot." After the apostle Paul was converted on the Road to Damascus, Jesus said to him,

"But rise, and stand on your feet; for I have appeared to you for this purpose, to make you a minister and a witness . . . , to open their eyes, in order to turn them from darkness to light, and from the power of Satan to God, that they may receive forgiveness of sins . . ." (Acts 26:16–18)

If you know this same Jesus, you too have the same commission: "to open their eyes, in order to turn [sinners] from darkness to light, and from the power of Satan to God, that they may receive forgiveness of sins." The way to do that is to follow the way Paul did it—the way Jesus did it. Learn to follow the biblical method of using the Law (the Ten Commandments) to show this sinful world why they need the Savior.

Satan, the God of all dissension, stirreth up daily new sects, and last of all, which of all other I should never have foreseen or once suspected, he has raised up a sect as such as teach . . . that men should not be terrified by the Law, but gently exhorted by the preaching of the grace of Christ.

—MARTIN LUTHER

VIEWER LETTER

Light at the end of the tunnel
You guys are doing an incredible thing. I tuned in to the program one night and was unable to take my eyes off the screen. I have wanted to witness since becoming a Christian but I have always felt unequipped or afraid I would say the wrong thing. With your teachings I actually see light at the end of the tunnel. I ordered the Foundation Course and am reading *The Way of the Master* book and will be leading a study group in the next few weeks. I live in a tourist town in the Great Smoky Mountains and have an opportunity to share the gospel with thousands of people who come through our town as well as members of my own family who do not yet know Jesus. Even my children ages 7–11 enjoy watching the program. I'm very excited to put into action what I am learning.

I am 35 years old and grew up watching "Growing Pains" and always liked Kirk Cameron's character. I was blown away many years later when I learned that he was now a Christian and would play "Buck Williams" from the *Left Behind* books. Having identified somehow with these characters at different times in my life, I find it even easier to enjoy learning from Kirk in this exciting way. Also Ray seems to have an incredible love that just oozes from him as I watch him witness on the program. I can't begin to tell you how much I appreciate the mighty work for the Lord that is being done. Thank you and God bless.
—Craig C.

Las Vegas

When the woman on the left was asked why Las Vegas was called "Sin City," her friend (who professed faith in Jesus) became a little embarrassed by her answers.

The Russian roulette challenge.

WORDS OF COMFORT

THE THEME OF this episode is that saying there is no Hell is the greatest gamble of life. On the program we reasoned that if God is good, He must punish murderers and rapists. If He is totally good, He must also punish liars and thieves—His justice will be in direct proportion to His goodness. If He is thoroughly good, He will therefore be thoroughly just. That is why the Law is so wonderful —in just moments, it gives blind sinners light. They begin by adamantly saying they don't believe in the existence of Hell. That makes sense to them. How could God, who is love, send people to everlasting Hell? The very thought is offensive. Yet, after a little reasoning about the justice of punishment for rapists and murderers, people nod in agreement that judgment is not only reasonable, but necessary if God is good.

Then in comes the light of the Law to show sinners that they also are guilty and under God's just wrath. They try to justify themselves—saying they are basically good—but the Law won't let them. They try to cover their sins with good works. The Law rips away the fig leaves of self-righteousness, revealing to them that they are guilty, exposed, and without hope. They need the blood of the Savior to wash away their sin, if they are going to live.

For many years I would watch the Law do its powerful work as I shared with the lost. I would think, *Wouldn't it be wonderful if somehow someone was filming this, so that other Christians could see what's happening?* That's why I shake my head in disbelief every time I watch "The Way of the Master." We not only have it on film, but it's airing on worldwide television. But more than that—I know what I do with a remote control: I channel surf. Most men do the same, and many channel surfers are beaching themselves when they see Kirk's familiar face, or when they see someone in a witnessing situation. They are stopping to eavesdrop, and are hearing a clear gospel presentation that includes the essentials of sin, righteousness, and judgment.

This Australian woman was very congenial and open to the things of God, and appreciated what she heard.

There is no doctrine which I would more willingly remove from Christianity than the doctrine of hell, if it lay in my power. But it has the full support of Scripture and, especially, of our Lord's own words; it has always been held by the Christian Church, and it has the support of reason.
—C. S. LEWIS

A cowboy is given the Russian roulette challenge.

This lady was in Vegas to gamble, work out, and sunbathe.

VIEWER'S QUESTION

"Ray, was it difficult to learn to do television? What are the easiest and hardest aspects?"

I had done a lot of video work in the past, but it is different on a live shoot. The hardest part for me is memorizing material. For a week before the filming I look at notes, use a tape recording, and keep reviewing the script until I feel reasonably confident. It is easiest when I am using material from my own sermons that I have already memorized.

A colorful New York couple.

VIEWER LETTER

Implementing the "lost key"

We are stationed at a U.S. military base in Germany. We attend a small military chapel with approximately 110 members, and God has blessed us mightily with a retired Bible-believing military chaplain who lovingly preaches from the Word without compromise. During the summer, he and about ten of us met biweekly to watch "The Way of the Master" series on evangelism. They were so well-produced, and most importantly, filled to overflowing with biblical truth. With each lesson, we became more and more burdened for the lost all around us. This has had a profound impact on us, our church, and this small community. Several people have already come to the Lord in true conversion as we have implemented the "lost key" of the Law. We have such a sense that this is just the tip of the iceberg of what the Lord wants to do in this German valley. There is no question that your incredible, 100% biblical resources and incredible ministry have played a huge part in all that is happening here. We tell everyone to go to your website and get your resources because they are so excellent and are 100% biblical truth. Keep up the fantastic work.

—*Rick and Lisa L., Germany*

LET THERE BE LIGHT

WHILE IN LAS VEGAS on a shoot, the crew and I were waiting in the hotel lobby to get our rooms. I'm such a coward when handing out tracts that I chose two little boys to show the pink and blue (Curved Illusion) tracts to. The boys were probably about 7 and 9 years old, had black-rimmed glasses, and were each carrying books—very studious-looking.

"Which one is longer—pink or blue?" I said to one of the boys. He replied flatly, "They're both the same! We have a whole book with stuff like that in it!" Boy, did I feel foolish. All I could think to say was, "Well, here, take these anyway."

When I looked over at Kirk, bless his encouraging soul, he called me over and asked why I was looking so forlorn. I explained that I'd just been brushed off by two "triple-A" students. Kirk just smiled and said, "Well, I bet they've never seen this before—I bet I can make them smile." Kirk pulled out the thumb lights and began to do his light tricks.[2] When the boys saw it, they smiled and were amazed, and I was very encouraged. Kirk and Ray are great to be around when you need encouragement!

—*Carol Scott*

[2] *The thumb lights are available at www.livingwaters.com/lightshow.*

Catalina Island

We filmed a couple of interviews on beautiful Catalina Island when Ray went there to speak. This young lady became tearful when she recognized her sin.

DISARMING STRANGERS — RAY COMFORT

MOST PEOPLE KEEP to themselves. They are birds of a feather and they prefer to keep it that way. But the Christian has another preference. He knows that he *must* speak to strangers—if he cares about them, and if he is concerned with doing the will of the One he calls "Lord." He has the example of the way of the Master—how Jesus spoke with strangers. If you study John chapter four, you will see that Jesus took the initiative with the woman at the well by speaking to her first. He had an agenda.

You and I have a clear agenda. We want the world to hear the gospel and to be saved. We have to go to them—we have to take the initiative.

You are in a battle for the souls of men and women, so here are some vital battle strategies to help you achieve the victory. The first is to *identify the enemy*. It is a demonic realm that seeks to intimidate you with the weapon of fear. It is meant to paralyze you. *Your* weapon is faith. It is more powerful than fear. Faith *overcomes* it. Your fear is that if you bring up the things of God, the stranger will think you are strange. He will think you are a religious weirdo. But faith gives you the knowledge that if the stranger dies in his sins, he will go to Hell . . . forever. Love for him and concern for his eternal salvation will overcome your fear. Simply think of this reality: your worst-case scenario is that you will feel like a weirdo. His worst-case scenario is the Lake of Fire, so you *must* make the first move.

The second strategy is to *be mentally prepared*. That will fuel your courage. If you don't know what you are going to say, you will want to retreat. So, formulate your thoughts, and think of where you are going to take the conversation. You are going to greet the person with courtesy—perhaps a warm, "Good morning," or "Hello," or another appropriate greeting.

The third strategy is to *be armed*. Always carry gospel tracts. They are bullets in your gun. If you don't have any bullets, you won't have any courage. You will probably be shot to pieces by the enemy. That means you will lose the battle.

Play it out in your mind: Greet the person warmly; that will disarm him. Then hold out a tract and ask, "Did you get one of these?" The purpose of the "bullet" is to get him to surrender to your will. You want to speak to him about the things of God, and the tract will help to get you there.

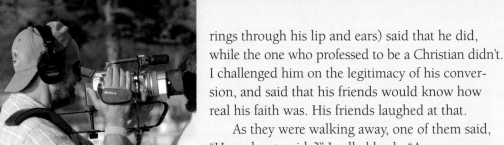

Remember to take control of the conversation. You know where you want to go, so steer the conversation in that direction. You can do this, with a little practice.

Perhaps the best way I can help you is for you to come with me as I relive two recent incidents that are typical of witnessing encounters with strangers. See if you can spot the strategies as they are used.

"Friendship Evangelism"
One Sunday afternoon I saw three youths walking along a sidewalk. I grabbed three copies of our Million Dollar Bill tract, walked up to them and asked, "Did you guys get one of these?" As they said a predictable, "One of what?" I handed them the tracts and said, "It's a million dollars." Two were evidently impressed and slowed down, while the third walked on. I had three coins in my pocket (they have the Ten Commandments on one side and the gospel on the other), so I said, "I've got another gift for you." That made Mr. Walk-on walk back. I handed the coin to the two who had stopped and tossed another to the third, and added, "They have the Ten Commandments on them. Do you guys have a Christian background?"

One replied that he was a Christian. The other two had no Christian background whatsoever, so I asked if they considered themselves to be good people. They did, so we went through the Law, into grace.

I asked if they had Bibles at home. One of the youths (who had

rings through his lip and ears) said that he did, while the one who professed to be a Christian didn't. I challenged him on the legitimacy of his conversion, and said that his friends would know how real his faith was. His friends laughed at that.

As they were walking away, one of them said, "How about a ride?" I called back, "Are you guys going somewhere?" They were, so a moment later we were all in my van driving to their destination, which was about a mile away.

We talked further about the things of God, and how I co-hosted a television program with Kirk Cameron. When we arrived, I gave them signed copies of my book *What Hollywood Believes*. I heard one of them saying, "I'm going to read this. *Really*."

By now I was on a first-name basis with Chris, Mike, and Malcolm. When I gave them the Million Dollar Bill, I had detected that they were short on *real* cash, so I asked if they were hungry. When they said they were, I gave them ten dollars. Then I did some sleight-of-hand tricks, which they loved.

Here were three young guys who fifteen minutes earlier were complete strangers, now acting like good friends, all because I had followed a few simple strategies to disarm them. When they got out of the car, they were elated. So was I, as I prayed for them on my drive home.

Red-eyed Rodney
Earlier that morning I was walking with Sue from our van to our church. As we crossed the road, a man in his mid-forties was heading *away* from the church building, so I took the initiative and asked, "How about coming to church?" He stopped and said, "I will go next week." Then he introduced himself as "Rodney" and asked me for my name. As he reached out to shake my hand, I noticed that it was filthy, and he had a blackened and broken front tooth. But what he

lacked in hygiene and appearance, he made up for in friendliness.

When I asked Rodney if he had a Christian background, he said that his mother was a Christian. I then asked him if he considered himself to be a good person. He did, so I followed with, "May I ask you a few questions to see if that's true?" He gave me permission, so we went through four of the Ten Commandments. As happens almost every time, he proved to be a liar, a thief, a blasphemer, and an adulterer-at-heart. How would he do on Judgment Day? He admitted that he would be guilty, and that he would go to Hell. I said, "Rodney, I don't want you to go to Hell . . . God doesn't want you to go to Hell . . .," and he finished the sentence with, ". . . and *I* don't want to go to Hell!"

I asked if he knew what God did so that he wouldn't have to end up there. He didn't know, so I explained the cross, the resurrection, and the necessity of repentance and faith. I then asked when he was going to get right with God. He started to make excuses, and talked about doing good things for people, adding, "I know that God loves me." People under conviction often try to hide behind good works or attempt to soften the seriousness of sin by speaking of God's supposed benevolence toward them. I asked, "Where would you go if you died right now?" He hesitated to answer, so I said, "You would end up in Hell, forever. If you walked away from here and your heart gave out, you would end up in Hell. At the moment you are an *enemy* of God in your mind through wicked works. You are like a devious criminal standing before a good judge." I asked if he had a Bible. He said he didn't, so I said, "Come with me and I will give you one."

As we walked toward the church, I said, "You may as well come to church." He replied, "I *promise* I will come next week." I told him

> *Give me one hundred preachers who fear nothing but sin and desire nothing but God, and I care not a straw whether they be clergymen or laymen, such alone will shake the gates of hell and set up the kingdom of God upon earth.*
>
> —JOHN WESLEY

that I didn't believe people who made promises. He then changed his mind and said, "Okay, I will come then."

As we sat down in church, I introduced him to Sue. He shook her hand, took off his hat, and joined in the singing. Then the sermon began. I was conscious of its length (some preachers give their congregations a taste of eternity). Just under an hour later, a red-eyed Rodney looked at me and asked, "What time is it?" I whispered, "He'll be finished any minute," hoping that I was right.

After the service, without letting him see what I was doing, I slipped $20 into the beginning of the Gospel of John in a copy of *The Evidence Bible*. I then handed the Bible to him, encouraging him to read John's Gospel. When I apologized that the service was so long, he said, "That's okay." He then gave me a heartfelt hug, and left.

Every church needs to send out a search party before each service. All they need to do is to watch for people walking in the opposite direction from those who are heading toward the service. The ideal would be to give them a warm invitation to come to church, but to take the time (as I did with Rodney) to go through God's Law with them first. All it takes is a little boldness, knowledge of the way Jesus witnessed, a friendly handshake, and a firm voice—motivated by love and concern for the person's salvation.

Again, love and concern are our motivation. Despite my hard words of warning about Judgment Day and Hell, Rodney's warm hug showed me that he understood my motivation.

Cerritos Library

Scotty sizes up the set for "How to Witness to a Family Member."

The director's view.

This shows the complexity of the lighting. Sometimes it took hours to get it just right.

EZ keeps an eye on the script to make sure everything is in order.

VIEWER'S QUESTION

"Why did you film in a library?"

In July 2004, EZ and Duane decided to meet in the Cerritos Library (about two miles from our studio) to discuss production. As they looked at the amazing high-tech building, they suddenly realized that it would be ideal in which to shoot two episodes, as well as a number of fillers. We made some inquiries and found that the authorities were more than helpful. The beautiful Cerritos Library cost $40 million to renovate. It was like stepping into a future century. We were so fortunate to have it as a location, as it was so close and enabled us to film in a controlled environment, at comparatively little cost.

Ray asks for an adjustment of the teleprompter.

Discussing the script.

Skydiver's Nightmare — Kirk Cameron

To film our episodes called "Evolution" and "How to Witness to a Family Member," we went to Cerritos, California, the home of "The Best Public Library in America," as named by a very reputable, national publication. It was a

truly incredible facility. It had all the state-of-the-art computer equipment, an "Old World Reading Room," an art center, a restaurant, and a "Save the Planet" themed children's learning center (complete with a life-sized Tyrannosaurus Rex). We had to film after-hours, so our workday began each night at 6 p.m. and finished at 2 or 3 a.m.

For some of our video shots, we crawled onto the roof of the titanium building and stood against the backdrop of the rooftops of the city of

Cerritos and a brilliant sunset sky. The tallest structure in the area was a Mormon temple with a giant, sixty-foot white spike on top. Ray pointed to it and said to the rest of us, "I know what that is—a skydiver's nightmare!"

Viewer Letter

"I would have been cast into the lake of fire"

God has changed my life through "The Way of the Master." If you would have asked me two weeks ago if I were a Christian, I would have told you (proudly) that I have been one for over 15 years. It wasn't until this week that I really, truly understood that I am a sinner and that I desperately need a Savior. I have been born again. I have watched your Foundation Course and have just ordered your *Evidence Bible* because my heart is breaking for everyone out there who, like me, thinks they are saved, but in reality are not. If it were not for you telling me, I would have been one of those who would have gone before my Lord and said, "Lord, Lord, did I not prophesy in your name, and in your name drive out demons and perform many miracles?"

Then He would have told me plainly, "I never knew you. Away from me, you evildoers!" I would have been cast into the lake of fire.

I am sitting here crying right now trying to find the right words to say "thank you" and yet all I can think to say is "thank you."

In just this short week I am talking to everyone I know (and don't know) and sharing with them the "real" good news of Jesus. I always have felt a burning desire to evangelize but never felt adequate to do it. Even though I have read my Bible and studied for years I never felt equipped, especially when asked hard questions. But you have shown me it's not about anything more than us understanding (by using the Ten Commandments) that we have broken the law by which we will one day be judged and, if Jesus doesn't save us, we will be condemned to hell. It's so simple and non-threatening (to me, too) that I am amazed. I thought I had to be like Ravi Zacharias in order to evangelize. I don't. How cool. I, too, can share God's news. By using God's tools/methods of witnessing, I am seeing people's eyes and hearts opened. It is miraculous and marvelous. I feel empowered now, not weak. Thank you again.

I will pray for you and I ask that you please pray for me as I go forth and share the gospel the way Jesus did.

—*Colleen C., Maryland*

"If he flubs it one more time, I'm going to box his ears."

Ron Meade (goofing around as usual) sucks his thumb during a quick 2:30 a.m. break.

A 3:00 a.m. snack between books.

Dale Jackson passes the time on *Treasure Island*.

Any man who declares children to be born perfect was never a father. Your child without evil? You without eyes, you mean!
—CHARLES SPURGEON

Conferring with the director.

I REMEMBER THE day Ray called me and asked me to pray about coming out to produce and direct a show called "The Way of the Master." Little did he know, I had already prayed—about four years earlier. You see, the first time I met Ray, I was so impacted by the ministry that I immediately asked the Lord to allow me to be a part of it, if at all possible. At the time, that seemed to be a silly prayer because there were no more than three people on staff, no Kirk Cameron, and certainly no television production department. But God knew exactly where I'd be four years later!

FROM THE DIRECTOR'S CHAIR

What a blessing and a joy it is to be surrounded by such godly men and women with a like mind to fulfill the Great Commission. I have produced several types of secular programs over the years that have been fun and creatively challenging, but I can honestly say, none of those compare to the joy I get from working a show that is changing lives.

One of the most important things to me as a father is being able to leave a legacy for my children. Although I'm not the one doing the actual teaching, my children can know my heart for evangelism through the biblical truths articulated in this series, and can be personally confronted to deal with their own moral dilemma when faced with the mirror of the Ten Commandments. "The Way of the Master" is part of the kind of legacy I want to leave my children . . . and my children's children. One that speaks of a desire to seek and save the lost. That's the kind of character I want them to remember in me.

Charles H. Spurgeon said, "A good character is the best tombstone. Those who love you and were helped by you will remember you. So, carve your name on hearts and not on marble."

—*Duane Barnhart*

Kirk witnessing to a "grandma."

We couldn't find a real one, so Ray filled in.

If there is anything in my thoughts or style to commend, the credit is due to my parents for instilling in me an early love of the Scriptures.
—DANIEL WEBSTER

Sue Comfort.

WHENEVER WE were filming, certain members of the staff would have to keep The Way of the Master and Living Waters ministries running—handling the mundane work of taking orders and packing boxes—while we were on an exciting location. So, when we shot locally, we liked to have our faithful staff visit the set so they could feel more involved in that part of the ministry.

Jacob Comfort watches the filming.

Ray and his lovely wife.

Daniel and Jacob Comfort sit in on the taping.

EZ examines the life of Buddha, from the library's collection.

VIEWER'S QUESTION

Ray, Daniel, and Duane.

"I've noticed the same rug in every episode, regardless of location. What is the significance of it?"

The rug belongs to producer Duane Barnhart. We originally intended to use the rug and the two chairs in every program. This was to create a sense of familiarity and continuity in the episodes, despite their being filmed in various locations.

VIEWER LETTER

Amazing transformation

I just wanted to express a heartfelt thanks to everyone at The Way of the Master. Last October you graciously allowed me to take your School of Biblical Evangelism course for free. It helped tremendously.

After spending a lot of time learning the principles, scriptures, and illustrations that were taught, I purchased "The Way of the Master" Foundation Course on DVD and took our student ministry through it. It was amazing to see the same transformation take place in the hearts and lives of our teenagers. At the beginning of the course only a couple of our teens witnessed regularly. Last week, 90% of our class raised their hands to state that they had witnessed to someone within the past couple of weeks. Today, for the first time as a group, we went to a public amusement place and used some of your tracts to start conversations with strangers. While many of our teens were a little nervous, they all overcame their fears and did a fantastic job. They can't wait to do it again. In fact, a couple of them went on their own to a local mall afterward to continue witnessing to more people.

Lastly, I'll say that I'm excited for the rest of our church. After the leaders in our church began to see what God was doing through our teens, they decided to have all of our adult small groups go through the DVD course as well. We're starting next week with that and I can't wait to see what God is going to do through our entire church family.

As a student pastor for over eight years, I've never seen young people or adult student leaders evangelize like this before.

—J. D. R., California

WORDS OF COMFORT

I ONCE DROVE home from out-of-state meetings having had only two hours of sleep. That's probably why I misjudged a corner and wrecked our van by hitting a wall in our parking lot. I should have thought about that incident when Sue said I shouldn't drive after filming through the night at the Cerritos Library and getting hardly any sleep. I drove anyway, and ended up getting lost on local freeways that I drive all the time.

Shortly after that, Kirk and I were on a major TV network promoting the second season of "The Way of the Master." He had kindly given me a card and a gift just before we went on-air. This was going to be much more stressful than a regular shoot—since it was live TV, there wouldn't be retakes if I flubbed it.

I gave one of the floor managers a copy of my new book *What Hollywood Believes*, and cleverly said, "It's written in a New Zealand accent." She looked puzzled, so I repeated the brilliant humor. After a third time of trying to explain myself, I realized she didn't understand what I was saying when I said "accent." This was because of my accent.

When I sat down on the live set, I accidentally bumped Kirk's notes onto the floor. He was getting ready for the camera to come back onto him and didn't notice, so I whispered, "I knocked your notes onto the floor—sorry." He swooped them up, smiled and said, "That's okay. *I'm used to it.*"

After the two-hour broadcast, Kirk came up to me and said, "Good job!" When I replied, "I was just praying that I wouldn't embarrass you," he asked, "Did you open the card I gave you?" I hadn't, so I retrieved it and opened it. It said, "Thank you for not embarrassing me. Your pal, Kirk."

The next day, my publicists called to say they had arranged a TV interview on Fox News about *What Hollywood Believes*. It was live and the potential audience was 89 million, so I didn't want to flub this one.

As Sue and I were eating dinner that night, I mentioned that Fox had offered to have a driver pick me up, but I had declined their offer. When I told Sue I was going to drive myself, she asked why I would do that. I calmly explained, "Because they may send some dimwit who has no sense of direction, can't speak English, and ends up getting lost." She smiled and said, "That sounds like you."

We had a sound problem with the first "Evolution" shoot (with Bambam, the orangutan), so we couldn't use all of the footage. This was our second attempt. Shooting indoors at night is much less complicated than shooting outdoors. In a controlled environment there are no planes, jackhammers, honking horns, flies, light changes, barking dogs, etc.

Enjoying coffee and cocoa during a break in the late-night filming.

THREE CHAIRS — RAY COMFORT

I WAS IN AN IKEA store, waiting to pick up three chairs for the new viewing room in our production suite. As I waited, I looked behind me and saw a man whom I was able to discern didn't like Christians. This thought was further enforced by the fact that ten minutes earlier he had stolen my shopping cart. I had put it to one side and waited in line at a cash register. Seconds later, he came along, saw that it was empty, put his goods in it and walked off.

Yes, this man was a thief and he was a Christian-hater. That's why I wasn't going to witness to him. I was too busy, waiting. Suddenly I remembered that I had been working on a new "The Way of the Master" board game, and one of the squares said that if you backed down from sharing the gospel, you had to go to the "Chicken Coop." I felt like a quivering cowardly chicken.

I walked over to the man, gave him a Million Dollar Bill tract and said, "Here's a million bucks for you. It's great when you get the change." He laughed, and I felt the fear leave. I added, "It's a gospel tract. Have you had a Christian background?" He had gone to church with his parents, and drifted away. I asked what he thought happened after death—what did he think was on the other side? He said, "Heaven," and added that he thought he would be going there when he died. He also said that he had prayed "the prayer thing." I asked if he thought he was a good person. He did, so we went through the Ten Commandments and it turned out that he was a lying, thieving (I knew that), blasphemous adulterer-at-heart. He said that he lusted all the time, and that he lived with his girlfriend. He also said that being a Christian was too "extreme" for him; he would have to give up too much. We talked about the reality of Hell, and that if he loved his girlfriend he should be concerned that if she died in her sins, she would go there too, because she was also a fornicator.

Then I shared the cross with him, and gave him a book and a copy of the "Hell's Best Kept Secret" CD. As he took it he said, "Perhaps this will help me get things into perspective." I said that it would, and thanked him for listening to me. He sincerely thanked me for talking to him.

A few minutes later the three chairs came out of the warehouse, and I felt like giving three cheers for the fact that I didn't listen to my fears.

WHAT'S IN A NAME?

THROUGHOUT THIS book you may have picked up on Ray's keen ability to mess things up. You shouldn't laugh too hard because, you know, he has been diagnosed with a serious disease. It's called "Footinmouth" disease and it's horrible when you witness one of these episodes overtake Ray. Believe me . . . I have.

On one fine Southern California evening, we were out at the Third Street Promenade in Santa Monica—a great place to shop, eat, and share your faith as we've often done throughout the filming season. During a break in the interviews, Ray came over to meet some of the onlookers. One of them was a well-built woman who said that she loved "The Way of the Master" ministry.

Ray politely stuck out his hand and asked, "What's your name?" The woman replied, "Sahara." Ray said, "Sahara, now that's an interesting name. What does it mean . . . BIG and HOT?" (You know, like the desert.)

This is just one of many episodes of Ray's "Footinmouth" disease in action. *Note to self: Never ask a woman if her name means BIG and HOT!

—*Duane Barnhart*

It pleased the Lord for the sake of His righteousness to make His law great and glorious.

—ISAIAH 42:21

The library provided plenty of colorful backdrops for our "fillers."

Churches meeting right now, today, are filled with people who are not born again, but the meetings are such that they will never be pricked in their heart, they will never be disturbed; they are going to go in and out of church every Sunday, and they will end up making their bed in Hell.

—JIM CYMBALA

Mark Spence and Kirk.

Carol Scott.

DEPRAVED INDIFFERENCE — RAY COMFORT

FOR MANY YEARS I have challenged professing Christians who don't share their faith by asking what they would think of a man who read a book while a child drowned beside him. I say that love couldn't do that. Neither can love sit on a pew, indifferent that every day sinners are sinking into Hell. In civil law, the crime of doing nothing while others die is called "depraved indifference." According to Bill Bright in his book *The Coming Revival*, 98 percent of Christians in the United States are guilty of the crime of "depraved indifference." Only 2 percent share their faith regularly with others.

John Wesley said, "The Bible says go preach the gospel to every creature. For all the effect that's had on Christians, they might as well have left that in the original Greek." Don't be like most Christians. Live to reach the lost.

William Booth, the founder of the Salvation Army, said,

"Not called!" did you say? "Not heard the call," I think you should say. Put your ear down to the Bible, and hear Him bid you go and pull sinners out of the fire of sin . . . Go stand by the gates of hell, and hear the damned entreat you to go to their father's house and bid their brothers and sisters and servants and masters not to come there. Then look Christ in the face—whose mercy you have professed to obey—and tell Him whether you will join heart and soul and body and circumstances in the march to publish His mercy to the world.

It is a sad fact that many within the contemporary Body of Christ are so caught up in worship that they have little or no concern for the unsaved. Others are suffering from theological obesity. They take in fat-laden calories, but never exercise themselves to reach the lost. They are pew potatoes. Understanding the Law would help them to understand the cross. It would give them the needed adrenaline of a grateful heart to get up from the pew of complacency. It would give them evangelistic muscle. Nothing causes Christians to develop in their faith like the exercise of sharing their faith.

Dallas, Texas

The question that produced such a variety of facial expressions was: Why was the man on the left (a professed Christian) out having a good time with his buddies, with no real concern for their salvation?

This was a "hot" interview. Both these men initially declined to appear on camera. But when Ray told them details about the program, one said, "I've seen that. I'll do an interview!" He turned out to be a "bitter backslider" (a false convert), who used to be on a worship team. At one point he cussed Ray out, put his hand up to the camera, and backed away. However, with the cameras still rolling he was coaxed to continue. He apologized afterward.

DIVINE DIVERSION

MY PASTOR was told by a life insurance company that his profession was listed in the least dangerous category. I think that's funny because in my experience, ministry is one of the *most* dangerous fields to be in!

I find it nothing less than God's grace that we haven't been attacked several times while out on the streets shooting "The Way of the Master" episodes. Let's face it, we're confronting people to see if we can appeal to their conscience. Even though we do this in love and without being obnoxious, it still can be offensive to those we approach. I have witnessed people getting visibly aggressive on several shoots. For example, when Kirk was talking with some gang members, one guy got in Kirk's face and had to be verbally restrained by the other gang members. At Ozzfest, a guy Ray was talking with was getting upset. Just then a complete stranger ran up behind him and screamed into the camera. The man quickly swung around and punched the guy screaming. I think his desire to punch something (namely Ray) was divinely diverted by the screaming music lover. I wonder...how do you think the insurance people would rate us?

—*Duane Barnhart*

This young lady became very *thoughtful about her salvation during this interview.*

Evangelism Boot Camps

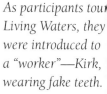

Participants in the initial Boot Camp, after their first day of witnessing.

Kirk chats with the team.

*As participants tou
Living Waters, they
were introduced to
a "worker"—Kirk,
wearing fake teeth.*

WORDS OF COMFORT

MANY PEOPLE have asked whether we have a Bible school on-site. We looked into creating one, but decided that other commitments left us without the time or the energy to make it a reality. Around that time we received a letter from Darrel Rundus. He was so enthusiastic about our teaching that I decided to give him a call. A friendship developed, and Darrel accompanied us on a shoot in New York.

While we were in Times Square I noticed that this man had a talent for rallying the troops, such as when we needed to pull every-one together and move to another location. I'm not exactly a giant and so when I tried to gather our crew from the crowded sidewalks, people wondered where the voice was coming from. Not so when you are six-foot-five. Darrel had everyone moving in the right direction within seconds. His strength of character and big frame, stomping around the sidewalks of New York, made me think of a prehistoric ani-mal, and earned him the nickname "Rundu-saurus." From that night on, we also called him "The General," and felt that he was the one who had the expertise to run a hands-on boot camp.

His faithfulness and leadership abilities were very evident at the first camp, and so Evangelism Boot Camps became a reality. This was just another example of God supplying the right person for the right task. There is no one like The General. I thank God for him.

Evangelism Boot Camps are usually held three or four times each year, mostly in Southern California. These camps aren't for those who are satisfied in their own salvation, but for those who are serious about seeking and saving the lost. Participants put into prac-tice the principles taught on "The Way of the Master" program. These camps truly are life-changing. Many participants have broken the "sound barrier" by open-air preaching for the first time. More information about the camps can be found at www.thegreatnews.com.

Brad Snow, "The Way of the Master" webmaster.

Daniel Comfort, handing out tracts at the courthouse (notice that they're all being read).

Darrel and his brother, Paul, sharing tears of joy.

Ray often gets carried away.

VIEWER LETTER

"What must I do to be saved?"

As I read through your book *Revival's Golden Key*, I had problems with what I was reading. I continued to pray about it, and I told God that this just can't be right. He spoke to my spirit and said, "Okay, find something wrong with it from My Word." My response to God was, "I can't," and God said, "You have your answer." So that's how I started out on what you would call "The Way of the Master."

I witnessed to a 17-year-old girl who was babysitting for my brother. As I began to talk about dinosaurs and how the world isn't millions of years old, it allowed me to tell her about the Bible and what is says. Then I began to swing over to the Law and continued speaking to her about her destination: Hell. I could really tell she was trembling before a holy Law. So with a glad heart, I gave her the Good News about what Jesus had done and told her she must repent and put her trust in Him. I also explained that this was between her and God alone, that she had to be honest with God and she would have to make the decision. Then she said, "But if I die tonight, I would go to Hell." And she literally asked, "What must I do to be saved?" I told her that if she repented and put her faith in Christ, she was also agreeing to be obedient to Christ and His Word. She needed to die to herself and live to God through Christ. This may seem a little extreme to some, but I didn't want to help bring a half-hearted person before the Lord. But by every indication she hated sin and loved Christ for the sacrifice He had made on the cross. I told her that if she wanted to repent and put her trust in Christ, she needed to pray and tell God all that she had expressed to me. With a humble and broken heart, she spoke her first real words to God, and might I say it taught me about true humility before a holy God.

Despite not initially liking your book and being challenged by God to find something wrong with it, a year later I have the honor and privilege to teach your School of Biblical Evangelism to eight on-fire adults who are not only being challenged and taught how to share their faith, but are also being challenged in their personal walk with God.

—Bud F., Minnesota

Witnessing on Hollywood Boulevard.

TRAVELING WITH A CELEBRITY: TRACT HEAVEN — RAY COMFORT

KIRK ASKED ME to accompany him on a flight from Los Angeles to New Jersey. He had been asked to speak to a large gathering of Salvation Army officers and those to whom they had been trying to reach. This would enable us to spend hours working on a new publication. Uninterrupted. Kirk would often come to our ministry, but other pressing things would pull us away from our work. This trip would mean 8 to 10 hours of solid labor. There was also the added bonus of his celebrity. Millions of people know who he is, so I walk slightly behind him and watch people's reactions. If they stare at him as he walks by I simply drop a copy of our Left Behind tract in their lap and hear them say, "I *thought* it was him!" Then they give me a sincere, "Thank you." The tract has Kirk's picture on the front and a place for him to sign on the back, if people want his autograph . . . and they do.

Instead of giving out tracts and having people give me a strange look, I have people lining up to take them. It is tract Heaven. The first time Kirk and I met, he was embarrassed that I gave out Christian literature. He told me later that he thought, *Oh no, he's one of them!* But as time passed, he saw the value of the printed message of salvation, and so he would often follow up my tract with, "Here's some *real* money for you," and give the person one of our tracts called A Gift for You. This is a lightweight cardboard tract shaped like a checkbook holder. Inside is a place to insert paper currency (of whatever value you choose), with a message that explains why you are giving away real money. It is so much fun to see people's reactions when they discover that there is genuine money inside.

As we took our seats on the plane, I warmly greeted the gentleman sitting next to the window. I introduced myself, learned that his name was Al and that he considered himself to be a "computer geek." I have found that if I strike up a conversation and learn some facts about the person next to me, I can easily bring up the subjects again during the flight and from there share the gospel. Al seemed a little taken back by my friendliness, and it disarmed him to a point where he became very relaxed and chatty. He was so relaxed, he used four-lettered words when conversing with me. That gave me a clue about where he was spiritually.

Kirk and I immediately began working on a book that we were both excited about. It was this publication.

A More Important Task

Kirk and I were having a good time and covering a lot of ground. But I knew that I had a more important task—I had to witness to a foul-mouthed computer geek . . . if I cared about him.

I turned to Al and said, "Kirk and I co-host a Christian TV program. Have you had a Christian background?" He hadn't. He was an atheist, so I asked him if he believed that any building could exist without having a builder. He seemed to understand my point, so I cut to the chase and asked him if he thought he was a good person. He did. I took him through four of the Ten Commandments and spoke about Judgment Day and the reality of Hell. Then I asked, "Do you know what God did for you so that you wouldn't have to go to Hell? He did something wonderful for you." He said he had no idea, but I detected cynicism in his tone. Earlier he told me that he had left his girlfriend a message saying, "If the plane goes down in a ball of flames . . . goodbye." It was that thought that convinced me to share the way of salvation with him, despite his proud attitude. I poured my heart out as I shared the incredible story of God's love through the cross. Suddenly he said, "Don't waste your breath," and he informed me that he had switched off the moment I began talking about the cross. He said he hadn't heard a thing from that point—that he had the gift of being able to tune out. I gently told him that the preaching

Ray demonstrates how to handle a heckler. Hecklers are the best thing that can happen in an open-air situation.

of the cross was foolishness to those who are perishing, and swung the conversation back to the natural realm.

There was a little tension, but it soon left as we talked of other things. At the end of the flight, Kirk (who had been listening to the conversation) gave him a copy of our tract called The Atheist Test. I wasn't discouraged by the encounter because at least Al hadn't exercised his tune-out gift as we were going through the Commandments, and it's the Law that brings conviction of sin.

It's easy to be discouraged by what we see as a negative response, but a negative reaction can mean that something positive is happening in the heart. Al was so convicted by the Law that he couldn't take any more, and felt so strongly about shutting me up that he risked offending me by telling me to stop. He has been able to shake me off, but if God saw fit to touch his life his battle was now with the Holy Spirit, and it's not as easy to quiet Him.

That night, before Kirk spoke, we spent some time in prayer and talked about the fact that each of us should witness and preach as though it was our last opportunity. Imagine that—if you and I could speak to our loved ones and strangers with the attitude of mind that we were to die after the conversation. Such thoughts tend to remove passivity from us. Kirk certainly preached with that attitude, and the next day we were up at 4:30 a.m. and on our way to the New Jersey airport for the trip home.

Too Early in the Morning

Around 5:40 a.m., Kirk was in line for a cup of coffee. As I waited, two airport workers stood in front of me, so I handed one a Million Dollar bill tract and said, "Here . . . you're doing a good job." He laughed and replied in a strong New "Joysey" accent. His friend smiled, so I gave him a tract and said, "It's great when you get the change."

I added, "It's a gospel tract. Did you see Mel Gibson's movie?" He

It was a great encouragement to see participants sharing the gospel publicly.

The police arrive, but let us keep preaching.

hadn't, so I asked, "Have you had a Christian background?" He was Catholic. "Do you consider yourself to be a good person?" He did, so I said, "May I ask you a couple of questions to see if that's so? Have you ever told a lie?" He had. "What does that make you?" "A liar." "Have you ever stolen anything?" When he said he hadn't, I smiled and said, "Come on, you've just told me that you're a liar." He burst into laughter, stepped forward and hugged me. It wasn't a brief hug. It lasted for about five seconds. *I had just accused him of lying and he was hugging me!* This was no Al Foul-mouth. Why would he hug me? I presumed it was his way of saying, "Okay. You got me. I have stolen!"

He then freely admitted to blasphemy and looking with lust. I said, "What's your name?" He replied, "Victor." I said, "Victor, listen to this. By your own admission, you are a lying, thieving, blasphemous, adulterer-at-heart. And we've only looked at four of the Ten Commandments. If God judges you by those Commandments on the Day of Judgment, will you be innocent or guilty?" He said, "Guilty." "Will you go to Heaven or Hell?" "Hell." "Does that concern you?" He said it did, so I took him through the cross. I explained that Jesus was bruised for our iniquities; that Victor broke God's Law and Jesus paid his fine. Now he needed to respond with repentance, and faith in the Savior. His friend was listening all this time, and they both seemed very appreciative at what I said. The entire encounter lasted about four minutes. Kirk was grabbing his coffee so I asked, "Have you heard of Kirk Cameron?" They had. "Do you want to meet him?" They did. Kirk then came over with coffee in hand and met Victor and his smiling friend. As we walked away Kirk mumbled, "It's before 6:00 a.m. and Comfort is witnessing already," and smiled. I felt smiley too.

The night before, we had spoken about what we should cover in sharing the gospel. The formula that helped me keep things clear was: "Sin. Judgment. The Cross. Repentance and Faith." Sin was covered by the Commandments. Judgment Day showed that sin had terrible consequences, and gave reason for the cross—God's answer to our dilemma—and the way to salvation was through repentance and faith. We tried to think of an acronym but soon gave up. It was a little difficult to pronounce "SJTCRF." Still, it was SJTCRF that kept me on track with Victor and his friend, as well as when I'm preaching to the unsaved.

Share the gospel simply because we have been told to by God, and because we care about the fate of those we love. How much you love will determine how much you share. Don't just seize the moment to do this, seize every second—it will never come around again.

VIEWER LETTER

"Deceived into believing I was saved"
Please keep on saying what you're saying. If I could be deceived into believing that I was saved, anybody could. I have read every book, gone to every conference (even spoke at a few local women's retreats), studied the Bible, listened to Christian radio from morning till night, taught Sunday school, fasted for 40 days, preached at my church, bought and listened to every tape available from Joyce Meyer, Jack Hayford, Charles Stanley, Beth Moore, Stormie Omartian, Chuck Colson, David Jeremiah, Dr. James Dobson, Dennis and Barbara Rainey, etc., have been a youth leader for 1½ years, and I still never, ever realized that I was a sinner and needed a Savior. I never heard it as plainly as you said it. The truth you spoke cut me to the core of my soul. What you said made me understand that even though I had done all of the things I mentioned above (and probably a lot more), none of it was good enough. I really thought it was. I really thought I was good enough. I really thought I was going to heaven. Now I KNOW I am. Thank you, thank you, thank you!

—C. Cummings, Maryland

A WORD FROM DARREL RUNDUS

As everyone who has attended a Boot Camp would tell you, the fruit that comes from it is nothing less than awesome. It's powerful to witness the way God works in the hearts and minds of those who attend. Watching people go farther and be bolder than they ever have before is a beautiful sight to behold. It's truly a blessing to see all the Christians setting aside doctrinal differences and focusing on our common cause for Christ.

Even better than the abundance of fruit produced during the Evangelism Boot Camp is the fruit that continues to crop up long after camp is over. I receive story after story of people who didn't leave their heart for the lost at camp, but instead keep the fire burning bright. Moreover, their enthusiasm for evangelism is contagious, and sparks fires in the hearts of many other Christians to seek and save the lost.

There are a couple of stories I'll never forget. One participant wanted to break the sound barrier at camp but wasn't able to overcome her fear. However, like a fire burning in her bones, she could not rest with her results. I thank God for burdening her heart with the desire to step up for Jesus because the first day after she got home from boot camp she took her husband and kids to a park, stood up on a bench, and started to preach to the public. She called me immediately afterward, filled with excitement and feeling vindicated. She now knew that God would give her the words, wisdom, courage, and strength she needed to preach the gospel if she would just have enough faith to open her mouth for the One who saved her soul from Hell. She's gone on to preach many more times in public places and is now training others how to effectively share their faith.

Another man went home so empowered by the Holy Spirit to preach publicly that he not only immediately began preaching in parks, he found a mannequin that he called Lazarus to help him draw a crowd in mock funerals. This pastor was so excited about the results, one Sunday shortly after returning home he brought the dummy up to the pulpit with him and preached a sermon on the fruit that comes from preaching the gospel. He is without a doubt a highly motivated, faithful witness who is serious about seeking and saving the lost.

It's like the boot camp is the launching pad for them to take off into a whole new stratosphere. I thank God for all the love, glory, power, and purpose He shows me through all those who have truly turned into a "nobody telling everybody about Somebody who can save anybody."
—*Darrel Rundus*

A passionate preacher—14-year-old Micah Brehm from China.

A pastor enjoyed the camp. Also pictured is Kirk's mom, Barbara Cameron. Barbara answers much of the ministry's email—a huge job.

During the early days of his career, Kirk and I didn't always have the most enjoyable or rewarding relationship. But nothing has made me happier and more proud than the relationship I have with him now because of our shared love for Jesus Christ. I am so thankful for Ray and everyone at Living Waters and The Way of the Master. They are an extended part of my family and I love them all very much. It is an honor and privilege to help others to become laborers in the harvest field.
—*Barbara Cameron*

Open-air preaching at Cal State University, Long Beach.

Praying for the man on the left, who just committed his life to Christ.

A Muslim woman hears the gospel.

Vonya Currie gives out a Million Dollar Bill tract.

CLOSING WORDS

Go into all the world and preach the gospel to every creature.

WE HOPE THAT this publication has been a source of encouragement to you, and that (as a Christian) it has made you feel that you are a vital part of this ministry. Although we may be separated physically, we are linked together in Christ. Each of us is part of the Body of Christ, and we have a common cause—striving to reach out our hands to the unsaved of this dying world. So never be discouraged. You are not alone. We love you and thank God for you. We want to stay in contact, so make sure you get our free email newsletter (sign up through the website), and keep praying for us, as we pray for you.

Until the trumpet sounds,
Kirk Cameron & Ray Comfort